AXED!

The 1980 Amana, Iowa, Ax Murders

by

Marcella Lynn Hatcher-Atkison

Copyright © 2023 by Marcella Lynn Hatcher-Atkison

All rights reserved. This book or any portion thereof may not be reproduced or used in any manner whatsoever without the express written permission of the publisher except for the use of brief quotations in a book review.

Printed in the United States of America
First Printing 2023

Paperback edition
ISBN 9798395188878

Also available in Kindle eBook

Disclaimer: This is a true story as seen from the author's perspective. Many of the names mentioned in this book have been changed to respect privacy as well as for legal reasons.

Note to reader from author: Keep on keeping on!

Scripture: "Be strong and courageous. Do not be afraid or terrified because of them, for the LORD your God goes before you; He will never leave you nor forsake you."
—Joshua 1:9

I have thought about writing this book for some time, but I questioned my abilities to write it and accomplish what I wanted to accomplish. I hope that as you read it, you can identify with some of the aspects of my life that I am sharing with you. Back in 1980 when this happened to me, I longed for someone who had been through a death to tell me that I would survive and be okay. That life had not ended for me too. My prayer and hope are that you have been inspired to say, "If Marcella made it through all of this with God's help, then I can too!"

Dedication

This book probably would not have ever come to fruition without the encouragement of the following people: Mrs. Kathy O'Brien from the Prosecutor's office in Des Moines, Iowa; Mr. Gordon Miller, the mediator of the meeting in Iowa with my email harasser; Mr. Mike Woltz, who has studied this case for years and was going to write a book on the murders but encouraged me to tell my story; my mother, Nellie Hatcher; and my husband, Vernie.

Also, I thank those friends who took the rough draft of my book and gave me their critique, editing, and encouragement to keep writing my story.

And last, but not least a big THANK YOU God for being there in my life circumstances.

May God give a special blessing to each person who reads this book and give them the encouragement to "keep on keeping on."

—Marcella Lynn Hatcher-Atkison

Table of Contents

Introduction by Michael Woltz v
Prologue The Road Taken 1
Chapter 1 God Ain't Taking Me Where I Want to Go! 5
Chapter 2 One Hand, One Heart 12
Chapter 3 Caution! Rough, Rocky Road Ahead 20
Chapter 4 Teenage Sweetheart: Roger Edward Atkison 29
Chapter 5 Rose 34
Chapter 6 Horror in Room 260 38
Chapter 7 A New Life 53
Chapter 8 Harassment 59
Chapter 9 The Elephant in the Room 70
Chapter 10 Person(s) of Interest? 74
Chapter 11 The Mystery of the Vega 82
Chapter 12 Feelings 85
Chapter 13 The Rest of the Story 91
Epilogue: The Difference 103

In Memory of:
Michael David Woltz
12/22/45 to 12/20/22

Mike volunteered many hours with the Iowa county Sheriff's office trying to solve this case. Sadly, he died before seeing it solved. His brilliant mind and compassion for the case will be greatly missed. Rest in peace beloved friend till we meet again.

Introduction

by Michael Woltz

Murder is nothing new. Taking the life of another person has existed since the second generation of humanity when Cain killed his younger brother Abel out of jealousy.

Now Cain said to his brother Abel, "Let's go out to the field." While they were in the field, Cain attacked his brother Abel and killed him.
—Genesis 4:8

The motives for taking another person's life are numerous and consist of human weaknesses such as wrath, hatred, jealousy, revenge, selfishness, greed, envy, power and control. Whatever the motive, murder is always wrong.

Killers come in all shapes and sizes. Killers can be male or female, young or old, wealthy or poor, tall or short, sane or insane, Christian or non-Christian, thin or obese, straight or gay, weak or strong and even a pseudo friend. We often think of a killer as a deviant man, hiding in the shadows and waiting to attack his victim. While a killer may in fact be such a deviant man, this is often not the case. There are killers who are known as pillars of their community. There are Sunday School teachers, mothers, fathers, husbands, wives, schoolteachers, business owners, school students, politicians and pastors who have been convicted of murder.

Victims of a killer are not limited to the person who lost their life. Most, if not all, murders have the snowball effect. Spouses, mothers, fathers, brothers, sisters, children, grandparents, friends and loved ones have to cope with the loss. We often hear things such as there will be closure once the guilty party is brought to justice. This thought is simply not true. After the killer is brought to justice, the living victims still cope with their loss and the murdered victim is still gone.

With today's technology, it seems as if no murder should go unsolved. While this technology often serves to identify the killer, there are still many murder cases that go unsolved. Much of today's technology did not exist at the time of the 1980 double homicide of Rose Zetta Burkert and Roger Edward Atkison often known as "The Amana Ax Murders." However, if the evidence was properly preserved, then today's technology can be used to provide new information and solve horrendous cases such as "The Amana Ax Murders."

Rose Burkert and Roger Atkison both lived in the St. Joseph, Missouri area. Rose, aged 22, was a single mother of a two-year-old daughter. Roger, aged 32, was a married man with no children. Roger and Rose planned to spend a weekend together at the Amana colonies located some 260 miles from St. Joseph. The Amana Colonies are a popular tourist attraction in the state of Iowa.

Investigators worked diligently to solve "The Amana Ax Murders" but were faced with many obstacles and many potential suspects making their investigation difficult. The murders were Missouri murders committed in Iowa. Hence, much of the investigation had to be performed in Missouri by Iowa investigators. Missouri investigators assisted with the investigation however, this was cumbersome because email, cell phones and other such means of communication were not available in the early 1980s. Adding to the complexity of the case, there were two murder victims thus causing investigators perhaps twice as much investigative work.

After years of investigation, "The Amana Ax Murders" became a cold case. This is not to say that the authorities have given up. Quite the opposite is true. The Iowa County Sheriff's Department and the Iowa Division of Criminal Investigation continue to do a full investigation of all leads they receive.

The current Sheriff of Iowa county was twelve years old when "The Amana Ax Murders" occurred. The sheriff knows solving a case that is years old becomes a little more difficult each year. "If you started to read the case report today and devoted your day to it every day, it would probably take you a couple of months to read it." The sheriff states "It's huge. Just to get to the point when you understand the case and the players, and the suspect of the day is quite a task."

Investigative agencies keep their files sealed from the public even after a case gets cold. Sealed files are understandable when a case is being actively investigated but it is also understandable that certain case information could be made available to the public after a case has been cold for years. Our society has a responsibility to remedy crime. Factual information serves to aid in shouldering that responsibility.

The intent of this book (as well as other intents) is to bring issues back to the table, rekindle thoughts that hopefully will jog someone's memory and thus provide information needed to bring the killer(s) to justice. There are books written and visual documentaries produced that have served to bring the guilty to justice. This case can be and needs to be solved rather than being forever elusive. For every mystery, there is someone, somewhere who knows the truth. Truth has but one version.

Prologue

The Road Taken

Scripture: Trust in the Lord with all thine heart; and lean not unto thine own understanding. In all thy ways acknowledge him, and he shall direct thy paths.
Proverbs 3:5-6

Iowa County Sheriff Bill Spurrier released the following statement Saturday night (September 13, 1980):

On September 13, 1980, two bodies were found in a room at the Amana Holiday Inn on I-80. The situation is being treated as a double homicide. Identification has not been substantiated and names will not be released until next of kin have been notified. The Iowa County Sheriff's office, the Johnson County Sheriff's office and the Division of Criminal Investigation are involved in this investigation."

I happened to be one of those *next of kin* that would be notified of this homicide. Have you ever felt like your whole life has been a dream or perhaps a nightmare? That you feel any minute you might wake up and find out everything that has gone on for the last 40 years was just one big dream or nightmare?

Those thoughts as well as others reminded me of the theme from when I graduated from high school in 1970. Our graduation theme was the Robert Frost poem, "The Road Not Taken," written in 1915. Here is the poem in its entirety:

"The Road Not Taken"
Robert Frost, 1874 – 1963

Two roads diverged in a yellow wood,
And sorry I could not travel both
And be one traveler, long I stood
And looked down one as far as I could
To where it bent in the undergrowth;

Then took the other, as just as fair,
And having perhaps the better claim,
Because it was grassy and wanted wear;
Though as for that the passing there
Had worn them really about the same,

And both that morning equally lay
In leaves no step had trodden black.
Oh, I kept the first for another day!
Yet knowing how way leads on to way,
I doubted if I should ever come back.

I shall be telling this with a sigh
Somewhere ages and ages hence:
Two roads diverged in a wood, and I—
I took the one less traveled by,
And that has made all the difference.

How could things have gone so terribly wrong in my first marriage to Roger? How could you date your teenage sweetheart since you were 15 ½ to have it end in such a bizarre way? How could you know someone for 13 or more years and end up not really knowing them? How could a Christian man who was active in his church stray so far from the right thing to do? He drove the church bus and sang in the choir. We sang duet specials for Sunday service. He was asked to become a church deacon, which he declined. Can you imagine being 28 years old, married for seven years, living a Christian life, thinking everything was okay, and then your husband is found murdered in a motel room with another woman who you have never heard of?

On September 12, 1980, my world as I had known it came crashing to an abrupt end. Roger, my husband of seven years, my provider, my teenage sweetheart and love of my life had been found murdered with another woman.

"He reached down from heaven and rescued me...." Psalms 18:16 New Living Translation. I was visiting one day with my childhood best friend from third grade Pam Yerganian Penland. She reminded me of telling her about my feelings after Roger's murder. I told her I felt I was going to fall off a cliff, and God reached down and rescued me. That conjures up some powerful imaginary in my mind.

Years ago, my life split into two paths that could take me in two very different directions. I had a conscious choice to make—I took the one less traveled. My choice: was it my *dream* or was it my *nightmare*? You see what an individual makes of it all can be *either* a *healing dream* or the very *worst of nightmares*. So, I would like to share with you how God guided me along this road that I have traveled. God *did not* turn it into my *worst nightmare*, but indeed it has been a *healing life dream*.

Chapter 1

God Ain't Taking Me Where I Want to Go!

Scripture: "That if thou shalt confess with thy mouth the Lord Jesus, and shalt believe in thine heart that God hath raised him from the dead, thou shalt be saved. For with the heart man believeth unto righteousness; and with the mouth confession is made unto salvation."
— Romans 10:9-10.

"The bludgeoned bodies of Rose Z. Burkert, 22, and Roger E. Atkison, 32, were discovered Saturday afternoon by the manager of the Holiday Inn, located just off Interstate 80 near the Amana Colonies, a community of Amish villages."
—St. Joseph Gazette, Wednesday, September 17, 1980.

My five-year-old daughter Corey and her four-year-old best friend Katie were playing in Corey's bedroom on top of her twin bed.

"Corey, what are you girls doing?" I asked her.

She replied in frustration, "Me and Katie are in an airplane, and God is simply just not taking us where we want to go!"

Out of the mouth of babes could no truer words have been spoken. It got me thinking that day and many days afterward of the gem that Corey had innocently spoken in a moment of frustrated play. Yes, Corey, many times in my life, God had not taken me where I wanted to go--but instead to where I needed to go. Looking back on the many facets of my life, I can see God's hand at work to mold, protect, and fashion me into the woman I needed to become and to be ready to persevere on the less-traveled road I chose years earlier.

I was born on May 26, 1952, to Floyd James and Nellie Anne (Hale) Hatcher in St. Joseph, Missouri. It was great to be born and raised in the South St. Joseph community, which had good family morals and values. Neighbors knew neighbors and lived in the same place throughout their children's school years and beyond. Neighborhood kids played tag, Red Rover, and many other games until way past dark. I remember the kids playing those games most of the time in my backyard.

I started kindergarten with a group of classmates and even some of us would graduate from the same college, Missouri Western in St. Joseph. I also started kindergarten with one girl in my kindergarten class, and she ended up being my supervisor in the school I eventually taught at for 17 years. That is something not many people can attest to these days with our friends and family spread out all over the United States and beyond.

I hated being an only child. There is a song recorded by Three Dog Night, "One Is the Loneliest Number" and that song is so true. Being an *only lonely* meant I had to have cousins and friends over to my house to play with me. As I was growing up, I spent a lot of time at my maternal grandparents' home.

I met my best friend, Pamela Fern Yerganian (now Penland), in third grade at Hyde Elementary school. We were locker partners through all five years (8th-12th grades) at Benton High School. We have remained good friends to this date, some 57 plus years later. Her daughter, Katie, and our daughter, Corey, grew up together and remain friends in their adult lives also. Something also rare in today's society.

It was around third grade that I remember developing a conscience concerning right and wrong. My teacher, whom I had great respect for, was walking up the aisle in our classroom asking if we had our homework for the day. I hadn't done mine, and as she approached my desk, I was trying to decide what I was going to tell her. I was feeling sicker and sicker to my stomach. She finally reached my desk. "Did you do your homework, Marcella?" I replied, "Yes, Mrs. Hall, I did." As soon as I told that lie to my teacher, I knew I had done the wrong thing. That lie gnawed on my conscience the rest of the school day and all night long. I just couldn't shake that horrible feeling of having done something terribly wrong. The next day I went to Mrs. Hall and explained that I had not done my homework and had lied to her. She was very gracious and forgiving, so not only had I learned my lesson to not lie, but I also understood what it feels like to receive forgiveness. What a wonderful teacher she had been to me that day! I now value truthfulness in my life as a very godly virtue. If a person can't be true in the words they speak, how can they be respected in other facets of their character?

One of my mother's sisters was very instrumental in getting me involved in attending church, becoming saved, and leading a Christian life. I became saved at a Sunday revival at the Second Evangelical United Brethren church around age twelve.

As far back as I can remember, music has played an important part in my life. At one time I took accordion lessons, and now I wish I had continued them. When I got into elementary school, I took clarinet lessons from the music teacher and continued playing in the school band at Benton High School. In high school I sang alto in Concert Choir and also auditioned for the small ensemble called Benton Singers and sang alto in that group. Back when I was in high school, some churches had youth singing groups that sang in musicals. I was in several church musicals such as "Celebrate Life" and "Good News". We sang the musical to attest to the Christian life we were attempting to live. We enjoyed performing at various places such as other churches and even at a nearby prison in Leavenworth, Kansas. Our church still has a regular choir which I like to participate in when I am able. I also like to sing solos for Sunday morning church. Many life experiences will bring a song readily to my mind, whether it be an old hymn I learned years ago or a secular song. Music reaches into the depths of my soul and helps define who I am.

Another important influence in my life from my early grade school years was being a Brownie and then a Girl Scout. I learned all different kinds of skills in life by participating in my Troop 141 and earning different badges. We got to experience things in our troop that I otherwise would not have been able to have done in my family setting.

Axed!

I remember a trip on a train to Kansas City to view a movie on a big screen. Camp outs on weekends or a week at a time in the summer. We had to work hard to earn money for our troop to take a trip to Washington D.C. That made the trip memorable for my fellow Girl Scouts and me. As far back as I can remember, I always had a problem with a very active bladder. The bus we took to Washington D.C. did not have a restroom, so what did Marcella do? I took my uncle's hunting porta pot on the bus for such a long trip. It worked just fine and accommodated my needs until it spilled, and urine went rolling down the bus aisle. Talk about embarrassment!

As a youth I was very involved in the Youth Fellowship organization at the 2nd EUB church, as we called it, where I met and started dating my future first husband, Roger Atkison. I was only 15½ when my parents first let me date Roger. Roger did not have a car at the time and was not allowed to drive the family car on dates, so we would take the city bus to the movies, walk, or ride his bicycle built for two. We rode his bicycle built for two all over South St. Joseph and that left me with a fondness for that type of bike even to this day. Roger's brother was supposed to have built the bicycle and it still remains in the family in his possession.

My first kiss from Roger, or any other boy for that matter, happened at my best friend Pam's house. She had a party for the Youth Fellowship church group in her basement. As Roger and I were walking up the basement steps, he took the opportunity to stop me and kiss me. I don't remember it being an earth-shaking experience, but it was exciting to receive my first kiss from him. I remember saying to myself and writing in my diary. "Well, you will no longer be sweet sixteen and never been kissed." And, of course, it was exciting to be kissed before my best friend Pam had the experience.

Roger would walk me to my maternal grandparents' house many times after school because his house was within a few blocks of their house. We spent a lot of time sitting on their front porch holding hands and kissing till way past dark.

Roger left for his two years active duty with the Navy in 1968. This was during the time of my Junior and Senior years of high school. While he was gone those two years, it was understood that we both could date other people. During the time he was gone, I primarily dated a very nice guy by the name of Hank whom I became quite serious about. He took me to both my Junior and Senior proms, and we also dated steadily during the two years Roger was gone. However, after he completed his active duty in the summer of 1970 and returned home, I chose to solely date him and quit seeing Hank. It was a decision that haunted me for many, many years later and a decision that I questioned was the right one especially after the events that developed in 1980.

After Roger returned home from the Navy, he resumed college studies, but college was a struggle, so he dropped out and decided to work full-time. I enrolled in the local college, Missouri Western State College to pursue a degree in Social Work. I was able to graduate with my Social Work degree in 1974. I was hired right out of college for the agency where I did my practicum, Buchanan County Division of Family Services.

On January 29, 1972, three important things happened. Our good friends had their one and only son,

Axed!

another couple got married, and Roger and I became engaged.

Recently, I viewed again the movie Sliding Doors starring Gwyneth Paltrow. In the movie the main character, Helen, gets fired from her job, thus making her return home earlier than expected. When she goes to board the subway to go home, her life splits off into two different directions. If she makes the subway, she arrives home and finds her boyfriend in bed with another woman, so she leaves him and soon after starts a new life and relationship with another man. In the other version of her life, she misses the subway, is mugged, a cab driver takes her to the hospital, and by the time she arrives home, the other woman has left. Her life continues with the unfaithful boyfriend through the duration of the movie until the end.

It is a very thought-provoking movie of how one life experience can completely change the course of one's life. Sometimes that life experience is controlled by us and sometimes, it is completely created by someone else and totally out of our control. But God has the control of it all. Yes, God was allowing me to go down a less traveled road that I later wished that I had not gone down.

"Dr. Stacey Howell, Iowa County medical examiner, who was at the scene Saturday, said the pair 'died a violent death,' but declined to be specific. He said there was no evidence of suicide, and that neither gunshot wounds nor drugs were involved."

—By Dix Hollobaugh, Mark Horstmeyer, and Vicki Shannon, *Des Moines Register* Staff Writers

Chapter 2

One Hand, One Heart

Scripture: *Do not intreat me to leave thee, or to return from following after thee; for whither thou goest, I will go, and where thou lodgest, I will lodge: thy people shall be my people, and thy God my God.*
—Ruth 1:16. KJV

Roger Edward Atkison and I married on September 1, 1973, at Frederick Boulevard Baptist Church in St. Joseph, Missouri. Our wedding invitations had the above scripture from the book of Ruth on them. During the wedding ceremony, we sang a duet to each other from the musical *West Side Story,* titled "One Hand, one Heart." The musical is like a modern-day Romeo and Juliet scenario of forbidden love. Tony and Maria are in love, but their love does not meet with the approval of their parents. In one part of the musical, they sing a duet to each other vowing their love for each other. They sing about making their hands, heart, and lives one and only death can part them. Thinking about the words to the song seems so eerie now. As if they were foretelling events to come in our lives. I had no idea of the road that would lie ahead of me seven years later.

Our honeymoon was a trip to a free two nights, three days stay at a timeshare resort at Fairfield Bay, Arkansas. It was the honeymoon that almost didn't happen. Roger was

Axed!

known to have a heavy foot and had received so many speeding tickets that he had his driver's license suspended and barely got it back in time before our wedding. Two other things contributed to a disastrous honeymoon. It rained the whole time we were there, and I had injured my knee in a college golf class, so I took sandbags along to exercise my knee while we were gone.

Our home when we returned was an apartment above my mom and dad's moving business, Bekins Move-All Moving office and warehouse. Before we were married, we had worked hard remodeling rooms in our apartment by dry walling and painting the walls to make it into our home. When we returned from our honeymoon, it had been raining back home also. Somehow the roof got damaged on the building, and it was raining about as hard on the inside of the apartment as outside. It took many trash cans and other containers to capture the rainwater. We had come home from a soaking honeymoon to a nightmare rainy apartment. Rain, rain go away and DON'T come back another day!

I graduated from Missouri Western State College in St. Joseph in May of 1974 with a Social Work degree. I was hired right out of college by Buchanan Division of Family Services where I had performed my student practicum. My job was Social Service Worker, and I counseled families in their everyday struggles and in Child Abuse and Neglect. It was a very high- pressure job as the child abuse worker was required to be on call nights and weekends on a rotation basis. When going out on a Child Abuse/Neglect call by yourself, one never knew what kind of irate parent you would encounter. I had enough of that and quit in January of 1978 to go back to college to become a schoolteacher.

During the time I worked at DFS as it was called, Roger and I purchased a big older two-story house with three bedrooms, kitchen, eat in dining room, living room, two bathrooms, attic, and basement in South St. Joseph. We bought this house specifically in the neighborhood it was in because we wanted our children to go to Hosea Grade School where Roger had attended elementary school and Benton High School where we both had attended. The house needed remodeling, but this was just the thing Roger and I liked to do. We were quickly immersed in tearing out old-plastered walls, installing new drywall, and painting to make our old house a home to reflect us.

After buying our house, we decided to start our family, but nothing was working out at all in that department. It was finally discovered that I had a female condition called endometriosis which would make it very difficult for me to become pregnant or impossible. There were many episodes of temperature taking to determine the time I was ovulating which would be optimal for becoming pregnant, but nothing was working. It is hard to put into words how difficult it is to go through such things as taking your temperature, doctor insemination by your husband, only to have a period every month. And to compound the situation, it was very disheartening because it seemed like every time we turned around, one of Roger's four sisters was pregnant.

Then there was the questioning of God, You gave Sari and Abraham a child after many years of waiting, Why not Roger and me? Even animals are able to procreate, why not us? Why, God, do you allow people to have children that they really don't want so they abuse and neglect them, even kill them?

Axed!

That thinking follows along the lines of, *Why do bad things happen to good people or good things happen to bad people?* I don't have an answer for that, either.

Finally, we decided to go the adoption route. We had friends who knew a minister in Idaho who was counseling a girl who indicated she wanted to adopt her baby out to a couple. We were contacted by the minister and started the adoption process.

Before things could be completed, though, a phone call came from the minister, who informed us, "My mother has had her baby but has had second thoughts about relinquishing her baby girl. She will think about it, and I will give you a call back as soon as she has made her decision."

We decided on the name Reagan Elizabeth for our baby girl. Reagan because I had liked the name ever since I had heard it used as a girl's name, and Elizabeth after Roger's mom. Those couple of days were some of the longest days I had ever spent. A lot of praying had gone on that God would see fit for the birth mom to relinquish her baby to us to adopt.

After a couple of agonizing days, the dreaded phone call came. "I'm sorry, Marcie and Roger, but the mother has decided to keep her baby. I wish it had turned out differently for you. I was just sure she was going to adopt her baby girl out to you two. I am so sorry. Please keep in touch," he said.

We were devastated. There were days of crying and depression on my part, but Roger and I never talked about it. It seemed like we had had this baby and it died. Finally, we were able to overcome this tragic loss and applied for adoption at the place where I used to work, DFS. In the meantime, to make matters worse, Roger's oldest brother and his wife adopted a baby girl. They already had three boys and wanted a girl. Then I questioned God again, *Why Roger's brother and not us? They already have three boys, and we have no children.* It was very difficult to accept their adoption and be happy for them. And my friends just kept having children, and here we sat with this great big house desperately wanting children. In this house where no children laughed or played. In our great big yard where there was no swing set where children laughed or played.

To somewhat ease our need for children, Roger and I hired ourselves out as live-in babysitters. We would stay in the home of couples who wanted their children babysat 24 hours a day for a weekend, week, or longer. Roger would go to his job as usual at General Telephone Company out of Savannah, Missouri, and I would stay with the children. I would do such household chores as mopping or vacuuming floors, dishes, laundry, and driving children to appointments. We babysat for doctors, business owners, and church families, and were kept as busy as we wanted to be with this job.

Earlier in the summer of 1980, we learned that Roger's youngest sister had become involved with an older, married man. She was only around 19 and this man was around 42. He drove the city bus and she became acquainted with him when she rode the bus to Missouri Western State University, the local college in St. Joseph. Roger was very upset with the situation for obvious reasons, but also because his parents had moved to Arizona and asked him to watch after his baby sister for them in their absence. An interesting side note to this story, is that his sister went on to eventually marry the man and is still married to him after all these years.

I could tell Roger was troubled by something that summer as he just did not seem to be himself, but I attributed it to his worries over his sister's situation. Because of sensing something was wrong, I looked him square in the eye and asked, "Is there someone else, Roger?"

After a long pause he replied, "Oh, no one in particular, but there are two or three women who live in the Savannah area that I could easily step into the father role of their children."

At the time I did not question him further as to what he meant by such a ridiculous answer, because I trusted in his being a Christian husband and his faithfulness to me.

A little later I asked Roger, "Are you considering divorce?"

He replied with a confusing look, "I don't know."

Divorce was not brought up again and he did not ask me for a divorce contrary to rumors. It was not until after his death and years later that I was to find out about other women with whom he reportedly had affairs.

Roger's peculiar behavior and the responses he gave me during our discussions, led me to suggest that he see a trusted minister friend. He went and talked with him the latter part of August. Little did I know what was coming in just a few weeks.

On the weekend of September 1, 1980, Roger and I celebrated our 7th wedding anniversary in Branson, Missouri. We camped out most of the weekend to save money, but we stayed in a motel one night. The weekend seemed to be pretty much uneventful, and nothing sticks out in my mind as unusual except for one incident. That night in the motel as we were retiring for bed, Roger took a chair that was in the room and propped it under the doorknob of the room door. I questioned him, "Why in the world are you doing that?" He shrugged his shoulders, "No big deal," he replied. However, he had never done that to a motel door before. And for goodness sakes, we had just spent two nights camping out in a tent. That incident seemed very peculiar to me, but I did not think much more about it until the events of the next couple of weeks occurred.

I would describe our seven-year-old marriage as very typical. Roger worked but was not gone excessive amounts of time for me to suspect anything. We were just like any other typical American couple working and trying to accomplish the normal things of buying a house, remodeling and furnishing it, taking a vacation now and then, and trying to start a family. We were both active in a local group we started for the rights of nonsmokers. And Roger was the Vice President of the local Solar Energy Club of which I was also a member. We served in our local church by both singing in the adult choir, singing duets, teaching Children's Sunday School, and Roger drove the church bus and worked at maintaining the buses in good working order. Yes, things were not perfect in our marriage, but I trusted that as a Christian couple we could work out anything with God's help.

We started a two-week babysitting job on Saturday, September 6 after we returned from Branson for a church family by the name of Paul and Ruby Black. The primary child to watch was their 11-year-old daughter. Two older college age brothers were also at home at the time, but they were not interested in babysitting their little sister, cooking, or cleaning the house. Roger left to work out of town at Kahoka, Missouri on Monday morning, September 8th. Roger stated to me, "I will be working at the job in Kahoka for the next two weeks including the weekend without any time off." Contrary to rumors Roger and I were not separated, intending to divorce. We even had sex the night before he left to go out of town for his work.

The only conversation I had with him that week after he left was on the phone on Wednesday. By all appearances, it was a normal conversation with no indication of anything wrong.

"The probe into the weekend slaying of a St. Joseph area man and woman in a south-central Iowa motel room remained under a cloak of secrecy by law enforcement officers today.

However, friends and acquaintances who knew one or both of the victims remained 'in shock' over initial reports of the slaying." *

In a few days, the world and life I had known would forever be changed. The road less traveled was about to get very rocky and almost impassable.

*Paul Stewart, Staff writer for *St. Joseph News-Press*, Tuesday Evening, September 16, 1980.

Chapter 3

Caution! Rough, Rocky Road Ahead

Scripture: But they that wait upon the Lord shall renew their strength; they shall mount up with wings as eagles; they shall run, and not be weary; and they shall walk, and not faint.

—Isaiah 40:31

I was on a babysitting job that Roger and I had started earlier that week. The 11-year-old girl that I took care of, and I had just returned from a day of shopping in Kansas City, Missouri. Her mom had hoped that I could help her daughter find a dress to wear for an upcoming wedding. The phone at the Black's house rang.

"Hi Marcie, what are you doing?" my mom asked.

"Well, we just got back from a full day shopping in Kansas City for a dress for her," I replied.

"Could you come over for just a little while?" Mom asked me.

This seemed to be an odd request to me as mom usually didn't ask me to visit during a babysitting job. Although I was tired from a full day of shopping and would need to start dinner soon, I could not dissuade her from the idea. So, I agreed that we would visit for a short while. I had the feeling that something was wrong and wondered what my dad had done now or if something had happened to him since he had a drinking problem.

As soon as I arrived outside of my parents' house, something seemed to just not be right. There were several cars present, one in particular I did not recognize. Again, my first thought was something had happened to my dad. As soon as we got out of the car, my aunt, mom's sister, met us and escorted the daughter away from the house. Besides mom and dad (okay, this was not about dad because there he was), there were two men dressed in suits whom I didn't know. Much of what was said after that is lost in time because I just went numb and was in denial.

I quickly learned that the two men in suits were St. Joseph detectives.

One of the detectives asked me, "Where is Roger supposed to be?"

I replied, "He left on Monday to work for two weeks for GTE in Kahoka, Missouri."

Another question by one of them, "When did you last speak to him?"

I replied, "I believe it was Wednesday evening."

Then one of the detectives dropped a bomb on me, "Well a body has been found in Iowa with his ID on it."

I was adamant, "No, that couldn't be Roger because he is in Kahoka, Missouri. Someone must have stolen his ID because he is not in Iowa. He should be calling me soon to tell me about the ID getting stolen and this being a horrible mistake."

The detectives were just as adamant, "Well it is a male body, and we are pretty sure it is Roger, and he has been found dead in a motel in Williamsburg, Iowa."

I am trying to process what they have just told me when they drop an equally confusing bombshell on me. "He was with a female by the name of Rose who also was killed."

"What? No! Roger was to work two weeks and through the weekend in Kahoka, Missouri."

One of the detectives asked me, "Do you know a Rose Burkert?"

"No, I have never heard of her before." I replied.

More questions were asked that were just a blur. I still believed that all of this was a horrible case of mistaken identity, and that Roger would be calling any minute to tell me he was in Kahoka, and he was fine. But evening turned to morning, and I never got that call.

I remained staying at my parent's house. After all, we did not know who murdered Roger or why. People called, people dropped by, but I remember very little about who came and what was said. But one visitor I remember quite well, the pastor Roger had gone to approximately two weeks earlier for counseling. Now since Roger was dead, he could confirm my worst fears. Yes, Roger had told him about Rose, and Roger was conflicted as to what to do about the whole situation. Rose had a two-year-old daughter which Roger had become attached to. So now that absurd statement Roger made to me earlier in the summer about women having children, he could see himself being a father to made sense. The pastor had warned Roger that if he continued on the road he was on, it would destroy him. The pastor was haunted by his prophetic words till he died. In his warning he was trying to tell Roger that the road he was on would destroy his Christian life and witness. He had no idea that in a little over two weeks later, Roger's actions

Axed!

would contribute to him losing his life in such a horrific way.

In my opinion, Roger's disobedience to God by having an adulterous affair with Rose resulted in God removing his protective hand from him thus resulting in his death.

Here are two scriptures that I feel can back up this belief: "Wherefore God also gave them up to uncleanness through the lusts of their own hearts, to dishonor their own bodies between themselves." Romans 1:24 and, "But whoso committeth adultery with a woman lacketh understanding: he that doeth it destroyeth his own soul." Proverbs 6:32.

But you may say, Roger is not the only Christian man to have done this. I don't have an answer for that. Again, I think of the saying: *Good things happen to bad people and bad things happen to good people.* That is where the *free will* that God has given all of us comes in to play. We can choose to use that *free will* for good or evil. Sometimes when we are rebellious to God, I think he just steps back and lets us reap the rewards of our actions as a parent has to do with their own child. It is hard life lessons and greatly pains us to see our children suffer consequences for their actions. I'm sure it is the same for God, but with him giving us our own *free will*, we may quite often stray down the wrong road. That road may be one that gives us great grief and pain. But in the larger scheme of life, it may make us better and stronger, if we choose to repent and learn from those wrong life choices.

Not long after Roger died, I was reading a Christian magazine about how perhaps God wanted you to remain single. "But God," I declared, "I was happy married. I looked forward to raising children with Roger, growing old with my teenage sweetheart. Why now am I thrown in this position from no actions on my part? The actions of two other people have forced me into this misery."

I went to my church minister for counseling. I told him about how I was angry at God for taking Roger away from me and especially in the manner it had happened. I often wondered why Roger couldn't have died in a car wreck on the way to Kahoka. That way I could have possibility been spared ever knowing about the relationship between him and Rose. Now besides dealing with the death of my spouse at age 28, I was dealing with being betrayed by him also. In one big swoop, I was now a betrayed widow, still childless, and with no husband to provide an income. At the same time, I felt guilty having the feelings toward God that I was having.

My pastor assured me that those feelings were only human. He told me, "It does not serve any useful purpose to deny the true feelings that you have in the situation that you find yourself in. If you don't recognize and own up to your feelings, acceptance and healing cannot take place."

This reminds me of a Bible Study I went to awhile back. The leader of the study had been through a terrible ordeal of her husband being in a motorcycle accident. He had to have several major surgeries for his injuries, and months later was still looking at more surgeries. She had to take a leave from her job without pay to be his caretaker. So, the discussion came up about questioning God in instances such as this. Several of the lady attenders thought it not right to question God. I spoke up and shared my experience of counseling with my pastor after Roger's death. I assured our Bible Study leader that it was okay to question God. That God was a big guy and could take it. Then that brings to my mind of the incident when Jesus was on the cross

Axed!

and lamented, "My God, my God, why have you forsaken me?" As perfect as Jesus was, he questioned our Father as to why he was allowing such a thing to happen. God is a big god, he can take our questioning. And then healing can take place within our soul.

However, my pastor told me if I came to him a year later and had not worked through those feelings, then there would be cause for concern. That was some of the best pieces of advice I have ever received in my life. Because once I could own those feelings by confessing them to God, I could then work through them and heal.

The months to follow were filled with much uncertainty. From the moment I found out about Roger's death, I lived back home with mom and dad. Since we did not know who had murdered him or why, I didn't know if that person or persons would come after me. During all of this, God and my mom were my rocks. There were many, many episodes of breaking down and crying, and mom was always there to see me through them. For anyone going through such an experience, one of the best things you can do is find a trusted relative or friend who you can break down in front of and cry at any time or place. Besides my mom, I also had a very good circle of supportive friends. I remember I drove to our house on King Hill shortly after the murder with some of my close friends and pulled up in front of the garage and just sobbed about how that house would never hold children for Roger and me.

The one thing I just could not cope with on top of all the other feelings I was trying to sort out was my dad's drinking. He was forced by mom to go to an in-house treatment facility called Valley Hope in Atchison, Kansas for a 30-day program. Right before Christmas, mom went down to stay with dad for a few days. While she was gone, I stayed with my aunt, mom's sister and uncle. We were going to celebrate Christmas at their house, so I took my presents there to be wrapped. I remember putting off wrapping the presents for as long as I could, because I did not want to celebrate Christmas that year. It would have been nice to crawl up in a hole somewhere and hibernate, and not go through the motions of happy holidays. When you have lost a loved one, the first celebrations of events are very difficult at best.

Dad came out of his treatment program before Christmas of 1980, but he was no more sober than when he went in. Finally, I told mom that I had not lived with an alcoholic for seven years and could no longer continue to do so. I was going back to live in my own house regardless of not knowing who killed Roger or why he was killed. It was at that point that mom decided to leave dad and move in with me.

I was glad to not have to live back in my big house by myself and that mom had finally been able to leave dad with his terrible chronic drinking and cheating on her. Dad did try to harass mom while she lived with me. One time he was drunk and ran up on the curb and almost hit my house. I told mom, "I am not putting up with him harassing you like this." So, I called the police. Mom was clearly afraid of my father.

My mother living with me, however, presented its own set of problems. The main problem was that mom still wanted to parent me. Therefore, she still wanted me to account to her for my coming and going, she would ask, "Where are you going? When will you be back?" or she would state, "Don't stay out too late." I had been

Axed!

independent for seven years and was not adjusting well to having to account to a parent again. I know she was just being concerned as a parent will be, but I needed to be independent and find my new self-identity. Eventually mom divorced dad and rented her own place.

An extremely important thing happened due to Roger's death. My best friend, Pam, had a lot of difficulty in her marriage. However, after Roger's death, my dear friend states, "It forced me to reconcile with God because I wanted to know that I would go to heaven. It definitely made us think of how short our time is and by the grace of God we better be ready TODAY." She and her husband were baptized in 1982, and they have been married 43 plus years! Praise be to God! I told my dear friend, "Even with all the suffering I have been going through, it is worth it to have you and Willis come to the realization of your need to be reconciled to God and to be saved."

With the above having been said, it is extremely hard to go from a married couple to a young, single widow. Especially when your close friends are married, having children, and busy building their own lives. I am not complaining or criticizing my friends, because they were very supportive of me. It just makes a big difference to go from married to single. Again, I found myself a "lonely only". I detested being a "lonely only" growing up, I hated being in this position again. "God, why have I been put in this position again of being alone? I enjoyed being married. What have I done to deserve this? If I'd have known the road I chose back in the summer of 1970 would lead to this, I don't know if I'd have chosen it. This is really, really hard God!" I lamented.

"The secrecy by Iowa authorities, including the possible means used to slay the victims has resulted in 'swarms of rumors.' This has resulted in the spreading of even more rumors and causes additional strain on family members who are in a time of grief." *

*Paul Stewart, Staff writer, *St. Joseph News-Press*, Tuesday Evening, Sept. 16, 1980.

Chapter 4

Teenage Sweetheart: Roger Edward Atkison

Scripture: "And I gave them eternal life; and they shall never perish, neither shall any man pluck them out of my hand."
—John 10: 28.

Roger Edward Atkison was born to James Harm and Ruth Elizabeth (Todd) Atkison on May 30, 1948, in St. Joseph, Missouri. He was named after the two doctors who delivered him. Two previous children had been born to James and Ruth before Roger, and four siblings after his birth. Jim and Ruth raised their large family in a bright blue house in South St. Joseph, Missouri. James primarily worked at the Packing House in South St. Joseph, and every summer, he put out a large garden. Both parents worked hard at their jobs; James at Swift & Company and Ruth with housework such as washing, ironing, and canning the summer produce. The children were also expected to work in the garden and obtain jobs when old enough. The Atkisons were a very frugal family that believed in using up things by wearing them out.

Roger attended Hosea elementary school throughout his primary grade years. School became difficult for him, so he was retained in the 3rd grade, which then put him in the same grade as his next-born sister. He and that sister looked so much alike that they were often mistaken as twins.

While Roger was still young, his older brother made a bicycle built for two by piecing two bikes together. Roger and his brother spent many hours riding their homemade bicycle built for two. This was the bicycle we rode all over the south side of St.Joseph, mentioned in an earlier chapter. That bicycle is still operable and remains in the Atkison family to date.

The Atkison family were regular Sunday church attenders and faithfully went to the Second Evangelical United Brethren Church. Roger was active in the Youth Fellowship group and was popular among his peers, being voted in as President of the group. He also was popular as a prospective date, as he dated most of the girls in the youth group. That is the same group from which he started dating me.

Roger graduated in 1967 from Benton High School and then went on to attend the local St. Joseph Junior College. His college studies were difficult for him, and he failed some classes. In 1969, he joined the Navy and trained as a hospital Corpsman during the Vietnam War. As part of his duties, he spent two weeks every year on a ship during his Navy Reserve years and two years of active duty at a hospital in Roosevelt Roads, Puerto Rico, working as a corpsman performing duties like a nurse. Roger's rank was HM3, which is an enlisted hospital corpsman, 3rd class petty officer. Upon completing his active duty in early summer of 1970, he decided to seek full-time employment after returning to college and finding it difficult. He worked for various businesses such as Blueside Tanning Company,

Axed!

Missouri State Grain Department, Bekins Move-All Moving Company as a mover for my parents, and he finally settled down working for General Telephone Company. He worked as a phone Installer/Repairman for that company at the time of his death.

Shortly after beginning to date him, Roger's mother made it clear that she did not like him dating me. Her reasons for this were never clear, but she did like the girl he dated before me. Because of his mother's disapproval, he moved away from home and lived with a couple that he and his siblings thought of as second parents. He lived with that couple until he went on active duty with the Navy in 1968.

As an adult, Roger was very involved in his local church. Before he and I were married, we worked as Youth directors at Frederick Boulevard Baptist Church, the church we were married in. Later we transferred our membership to King Hill Baptist Church, a church closer to our home in the south part of St. Joseph, Missouri. Roger and I sang in the adult choir, sang duet specials on Sunday, and taught Children's Church there. He also sang in the Concert Choir in high school and played the piano. Both of us were regular Sunday School attendees, and we were active in our class socials.

We were both instrumental in initiating the beginning of the St. Joseph Nonsmoker's Rights Club. This group was concerned with people smoking indoors and the ill effects of smoking on nonsmokers. We also were active in the St. Joseph Solar Energy club, with Roger being Vice President of that organization.

Roger liked to stay busy and was good at working with his hands. He and I remodeled several rooms of our old two-story house. He also liked to follow in his parents' footsteps by planting a garden every year, and I would freeze and can the produce he would harvest.

We liked to venture out and visit different states. We went to Los Angeles, California, where we stopped at Disneyland, to Washington, D.C., and to Idaho to visit his oldest sister and family. We were young, so pitching a tent and camping out on vacations was an adventure that we enjoyed. Since he was very frugal like his parents, this was a way to have a vacation and still be thrifty.

We entertained by having friends and family over for a meal and playing such games as UNO and Water Works. We spent many weekends entertaining friends or his sisters and their husbands at our house or going to their houses. Family was clearly important to both of us, and since I had no siblings to speak of, entertaining his family in our home was important to me.

We had several adventures with one of his sisters and her husband. One afternoon we took their boat and went up the Missouri River to Rulo, Nebraska, ate lunch, then came back. When Roger's childhood friend and his wife were in town visiting family, they would always make time to come to our house to have a meal, play board or card games, and visit. Our lives just consisted of ordinary activities like most couples our age.

"A South Side resident who was acquainted with the victim told The News-Press: 'I didn't really know him all that well. But whenever I did see him, he always spoke and seemed to be very polite. I knew he was an active church person.'" *

A close friend of the Atkisons, as well as other friends and siblings, described Roger as a good person, full of love, passive, kind, and soft-spoken. Roger did not drink, smoke, or cuss. Investigators could not get anyone to give derogatory information on Roger except for some references to possible affairs, and they could not find any mention of any enemies. He truly fit the image of the All-American Good Guy.

After Roger's death, I asked his closest male friends if he had ever mentioned any unhappiness with our marriage or his involvement with Rose. None of them said they had. I had asked this question of them because several newspaper articles had reported that Roger and Rose's affair was common knowledge "in the victims' community" and "not a well-kept secret." Still, it came as a shock to his close male friends that I asked and to most family and other close friends.

*Paul Stewart, Staff Writer, St. Joseph Gazette, Tuesday Evening, September 16, 1980.

When my road divided, I chose to go down the path of life with Roger rather than the other young man I dated steadily during my Junior and Senior years of High School. On that path, I incurred much suffering.

Chapter 5

Rose

Scripture: "For all have sinned and come short of the glory of God. Being justified freely by his grace through the redemption that is in Christ Jesus."
—Romans 3:23-24.

In talking with a couple of Rose's friends, they stated that Rose was a saved person. I hope that was the case. That said, we all are sinners saved by Jesus Christ's blood that He shed on Calvary for our sins. We all sin, most likely daily, and Jesus is there to forgive and cleanse us from all our unrighteousness.

An important event happened on Wednesday, May 21, 1958, in the life of Frank and Mary Burkert. They were blessed with a beautiful baby girl they named Rose Zetta Burkert. The Burkert family was a typical Midwest family of the 1950s, raising the family in St. Joseph and the Savannah, Missouri, area. Mary was a stay-at-home mom, while Frank worked hard to provide for his family. Rose had three sisters and four brothers. Mr. Burkert eventually divorced Mary and married Beth. Frank and Beth finished raising Rose and her siblings. Frank died in 1978, and Rose's brother died in 1977.

Axed!

Rose attended some of her grade school years in St. Joseph, Missouri, and later in Savannah, Missouri, where she graduated from Savannah High School in 1976.

At the time of her death, Rose and her two-year-old daughter lived in rural St. Joseph in Andrew County. For the three years prior to her death, Rose worked as a nurse's aide at La Verna Village Nursing Home in Savannah, Missouri. She had just terminated her employment there to pursue a career in nursing.

After Rose's murder, her daughter was adopted by a brother and his wife who lived in another state. Rose's daughter has gone on to marry and have a family of her own.

According to several people, Rose was afraid of someone and confided that fact to them. On Tuesday, September 9, 1980, Rose went to her sister's house and told her that if something happened to her, she wanted her brother, who lived in another state, to raise her daughter. She also went to law enforcement in Savannah and St. Joseph and told them if something happened to her, it would be her ex-boyfriend, David (name changed). He and Rose lived together for several months until she threw him out for his illegal drug use sometime in early 1980. Rose feared him because she felt he was stalking her and thought he may have killed her dog.

A friend gave similar statements to an Iowa DCI agent. In her conversations with the agent, the friend stated that she went riding with her in Rose's car about a week to a week and a half before the murder. Rose told her that someone was watching her house and that they had a blue car, and she was scared. She then said it was the first time she had been scared living in the country and that she didn't want to go home.

The friend was asked what she had heard about the murders. She stated that she'd heard that one guy, in particular, by the name of Randy (name changed), could have had something to do with it. She had heard this information from several sources. She thought he ran a dating service that was not reputable.

When friends were interviewed on their memories of Rose, most everyone came to the consensus that she was fun

Rose's Obituary:

"Miss Rose Z. Burkert, 22, Route 3, was found dead Saturday in a motel room near Williamsburg, Iowa. She was born in St. Joseph and lived here all of her life. For the past three years, she had been employed as a nurse's aide at LaVerna Village in Savannah, Mo. Miss Burkert was preceded in death by her father in 1978 and one brother in 1977. She is survived by a daughter of the home; her mother; her stepmother; three sisters; three brothers; and aunts, uncles, and cousins.

Services will be Wednesday at 1:30 p.m. at Meierhoffer-FleemanChapel. Burial will be in Memorial Park Cemetery.

*

I wish I could shed additional light on Rose's life, but I could not find any of her relatives who would speak about her to me. They prefer the "murder stuff" to remain in their past.

And one last thing I would like to say here on the issue of Rose. To set the record straight and stop one of the many rumors, I did go to the funeral home to view Rose's body to see what she looked like because, to the best of my knowledge, I had never seen her before that time. But I did not attend her funeral.

As a point of interest, some time back, a Facebook page was started by a friend for Rose titled, "Justice for Rosie."

Chapter 6

Horror in Room 260

"I, the Lord, search the heart, I test the mind. Even to give every man according to his ways, according to the fruit of his doings." Jeremiah 17:10

On September 12, 1980, my world as I knew it ceased to be. As of that date, I was no longer a wife but a 28-year-old widow. My world had forever changed. I wondered again, *had I chosen the wrong path years ago?*

The housekeeper went to room 260 to do her routine cleaning at around 1:00 p.m. She unlocked the door and went inside, even though a *"Do Not Disturb"* sign hung outside. The television was on, and some of the guests' belongings were still there. As she ventured farther into the room, the sight that caught her eyes was too grisly and horrendous for her to comprehend. She quickly turned and left, hurrying to the motel manager on duty.

Before Roger left for work on Monday, September 8, he told me he had to work for two weeks, including the weekend in between, in Kahoka, Missouri. It was a typical business trip for the phone company he worked for, GTE. On September 13, I was notified that he had been murdered with his girlfriend, Rose Burkert, in a Holiday Inn in Williamsburg, Iowa, off I-80.

I was unaware of his infidelity, so I not only had to process his death by murder but also a betrayal by my

Axed!

spouse of seven years, who had also been my teenage sweetheart since I was 15½ years old.

The details of the murder have mostly been gleaned from newspaper articles since law enforcement seemed closed mouth on many of the specifics. I ended up hiring a private investigator to help bring to light at least some of those details for me. I learned that Rose was an unwed mother of a two-year-old daughter. She had worked at a nursing home in the same town where Roger's job was located, Savannah, Missouri. Rose was to start nursing school when she returned from the weekend with my husband.

She met Roger in June of 1980 when he did some telephone work for her in her home. That was likely when the affair started.

Rose had driven to Kahoka on Wednesday of that week and had stayed with Roger the rest of the week in the motel room provided by his employer. Rose had introduced herself to the motel personnel as Roger's wife.

When he got off work on Friday, September 12, together they headed for the Amana Colonies in Iowa near Williamsburg for the weekend. They traveled up U.S. Highway 218 and Interstate 80 between 5:00 and 7:30 p.m. in Rose's 1977 blue, four-door Chevrolet Malibu with Missouri license plate PJJ-1012.

A mortician convention that weekend left the Holiday Inn with no rooms available, except for one cancellation. Roger and Rose secured room 260 under the name of Roger Burkert. They checked in at approximately 7:40 p.m. and were supposedly not seen again after that time.

At around 8:00 p.m., Rose called her babysitter. The babysitter's husband answered and said he would have his wife return the phone call when she came back home from doing the laundry. But when the babysitter phoned back at approximately 8:30, the call to room 260 went unanswered. Was this because the killer or *killers* were already there in the room?

The report states that three calls were made from or to room 260: Rose's call to the babysitter, the babysitter's call back to the room, and an unidentified third call to the room. Who placed that third call and why?

Upon arriving at the motel, the car was parked in a handicap-accessible parking spot to the side, near the back. Investigators speculated that Rose, who was fully clothed except for being barefoot, may have gone to move the car out of the handicapped parking space. But her task was never accomplished, as her vehicle was found still parked there after their bodies were discovered. Speculation was that Rose remained dressed to move the car but was accosted before she could accomplish that task. This could explain several things: the fact that she was dressed, and Roger wasn't, how the murderer(s) knew their room number, and how it was that they'd gained entry since there was no evidence of the door into the room being forced.

Since there was no forced entry, it was believed that the perpetrator(s) were let inside, possibly by someone they knew. So, if Rose did indeed go to the car, could someone have followed her back to the room and then pushed their way in as she reentered? Or, after she returned to the room, could she have failed to lock the door—could the lock have been faulty?

The weapon used by the perpetrator has been controversial. News reports speculated it had been an ax or hatchet-type instrument. But when Roger's brother, identified his body, he stated it was not an ax-type instrument. One newspaper article stated that Roger's and Rose's heads were split open by multiple blows from a sharp ax-like item with a 3½-inch blade, which may have been a roofer's hatchet or a type of machete. The blows were administered to the back of their heads as they lay face down on the bed. Death would have occurred in minutes.

The perpetrator(s) appeared to have spent some time in room 260 with their victims. Very unusual clues were left in the room. Two chairs had been pulled up to one side of the bed, the side that Roger was found on, as if a conversation had occurred between the victims and the killer(s). It appeared that someone had put their feet on the bedside nightstand. Soap shavings were found beside one of the chairs, indicating someone had whittled on the motel soap while sitting in the chair and then used the soap to write a message on the back of the bathroom door. All of that message had been erased except for the word "this." Toothpaste was also splattered in the sink and tub. The toothpaste tube appeared to have been smashed with a fist. A towel with blood on it lay partially in the sink, indicating the killer washed after the murder. Blood DNA found on the towel belonged to one or both of the victims and an unknown male person—more than likely the killer. A broken foreign object was found in the room, possibly coming from something like a chair, but investigators were unable to trace it to anything in the room.

Roger was found face down only in his underwear on the right side of the bed, partially covered, and Rose was found face up, fully clothed except for shoes and socks, and covered up more. The wall, headboard, carpet, and even ceiling had blood and pieces of their brains splattered on it.

Not only was the back of Roger's head bashed in, but he had several fingers on his hand mutilated as if he tried to lessen the blows to his head.

graphic for the Cedar Rapids Gazette by Greg Good from a DCI sketch

Axed!

Front of Building

Marcella Lynn Hatcher-Atkison

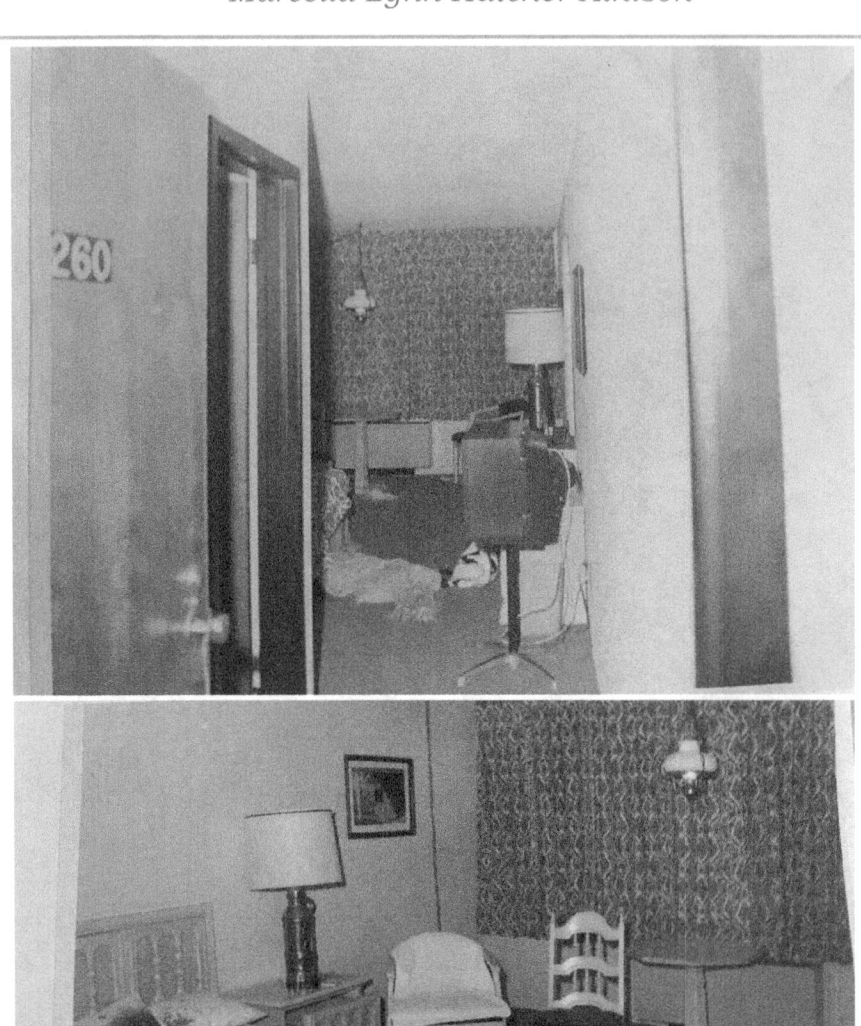

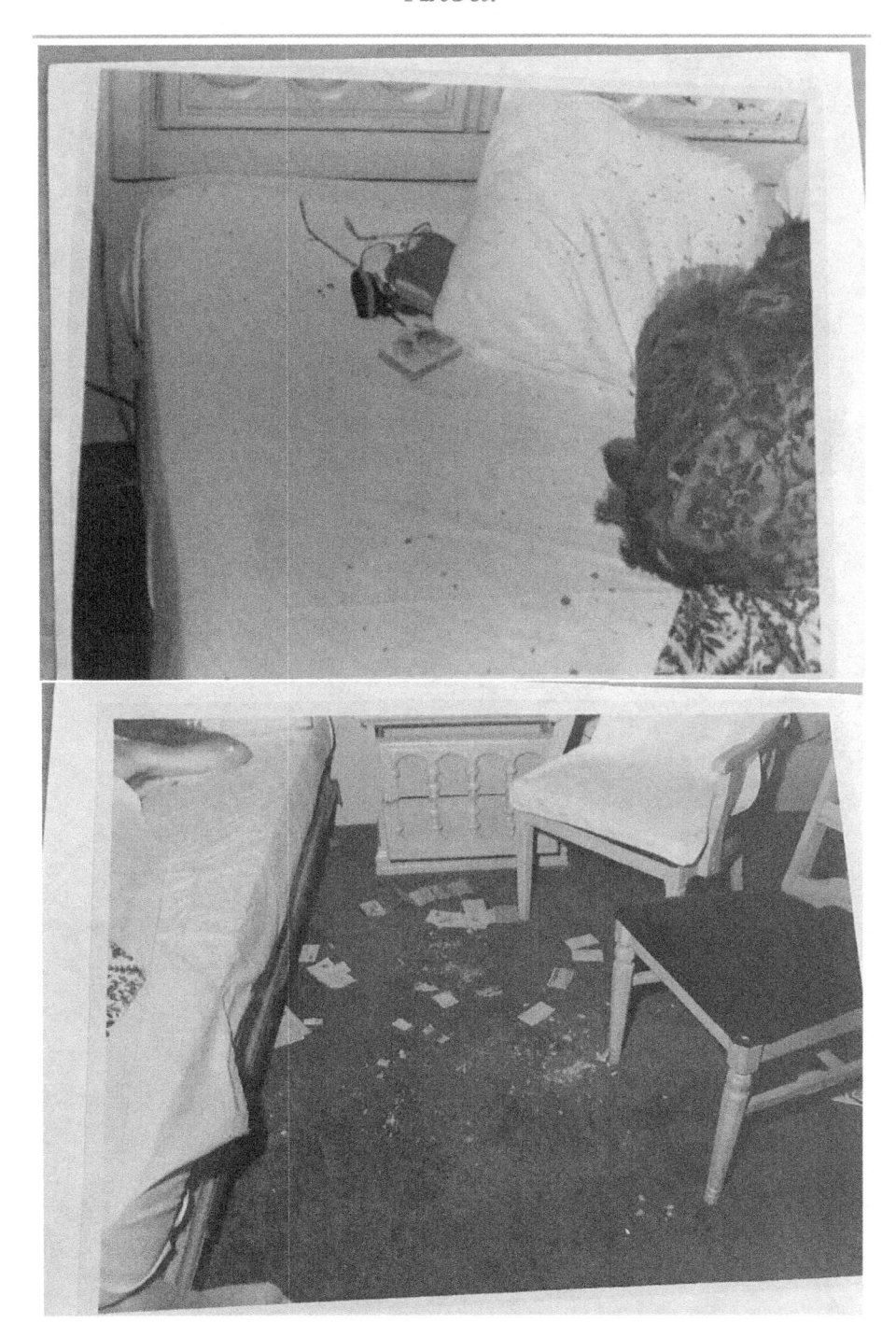

Axed!

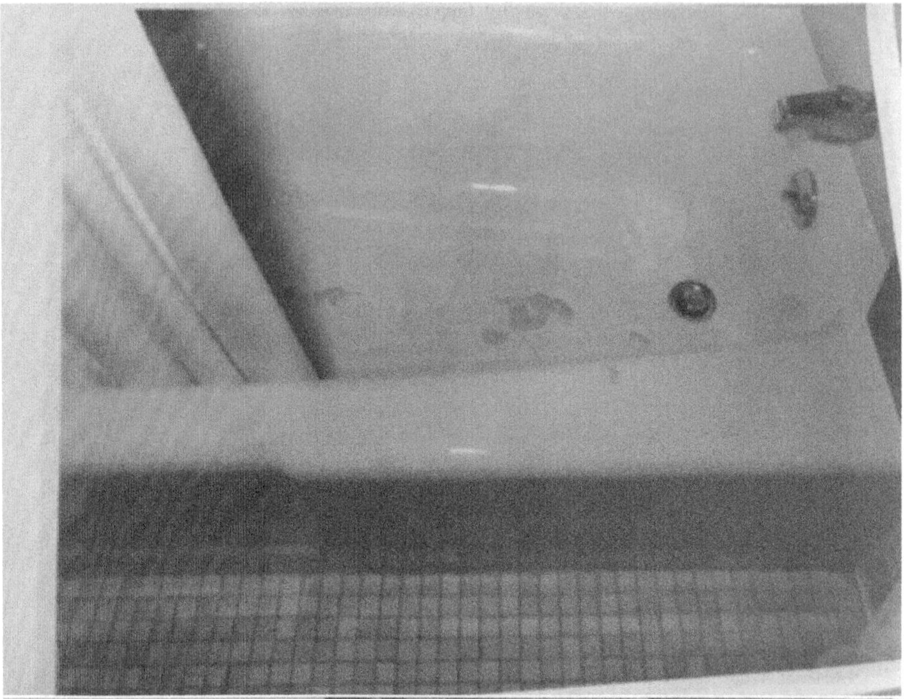

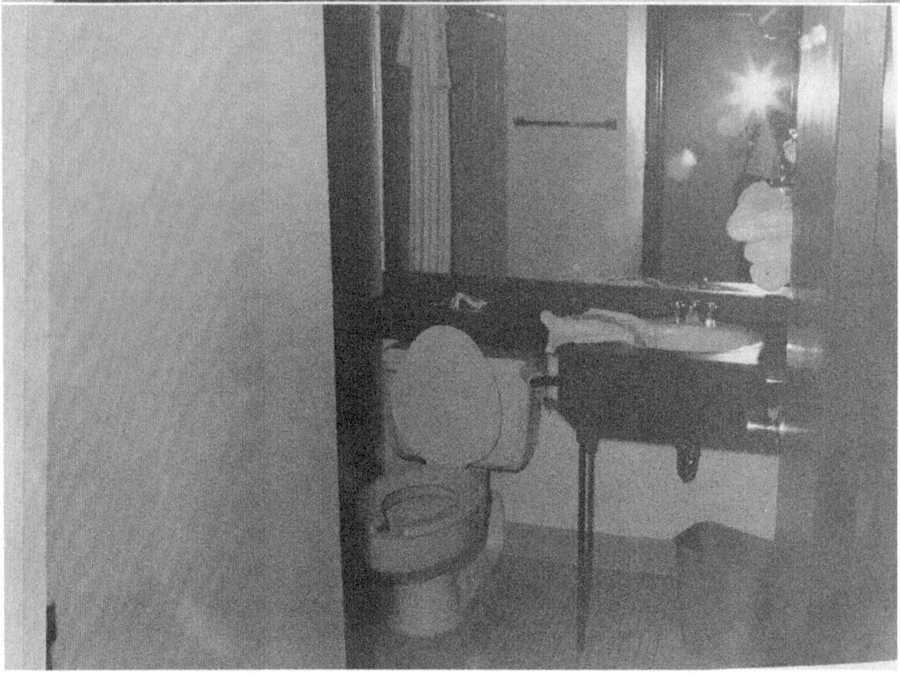

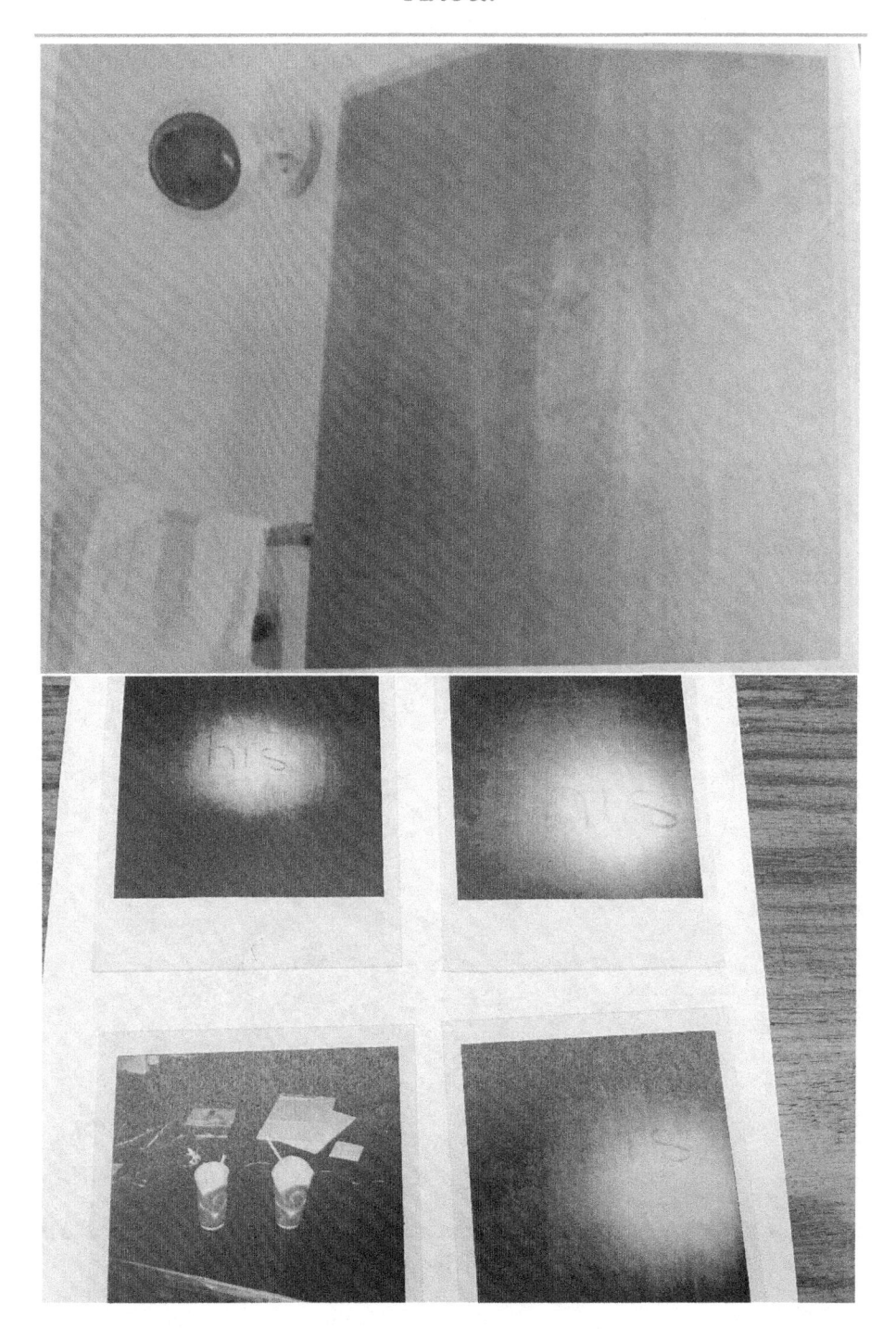

Axed!

Autopsy diagrams of the injuries of Roger's head and hands:

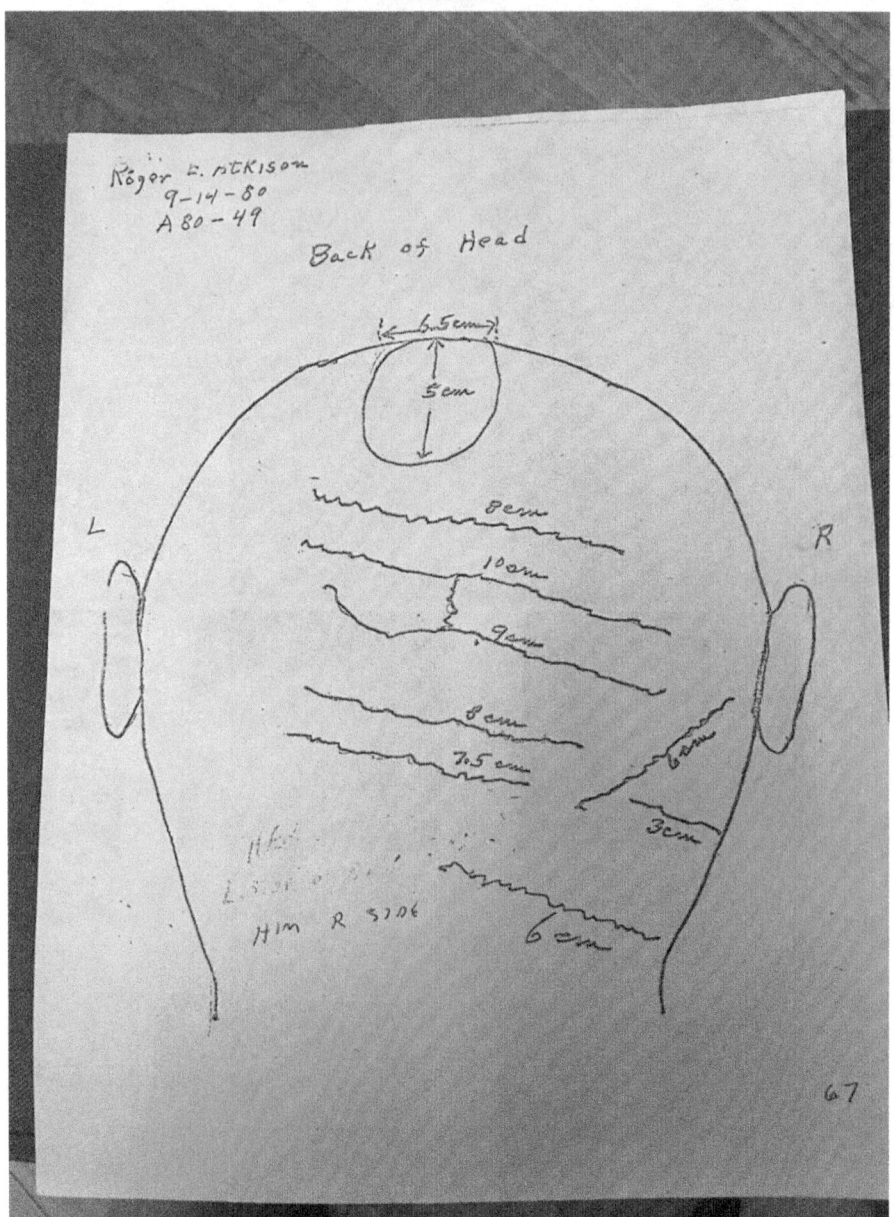

The Back of Roger's Head

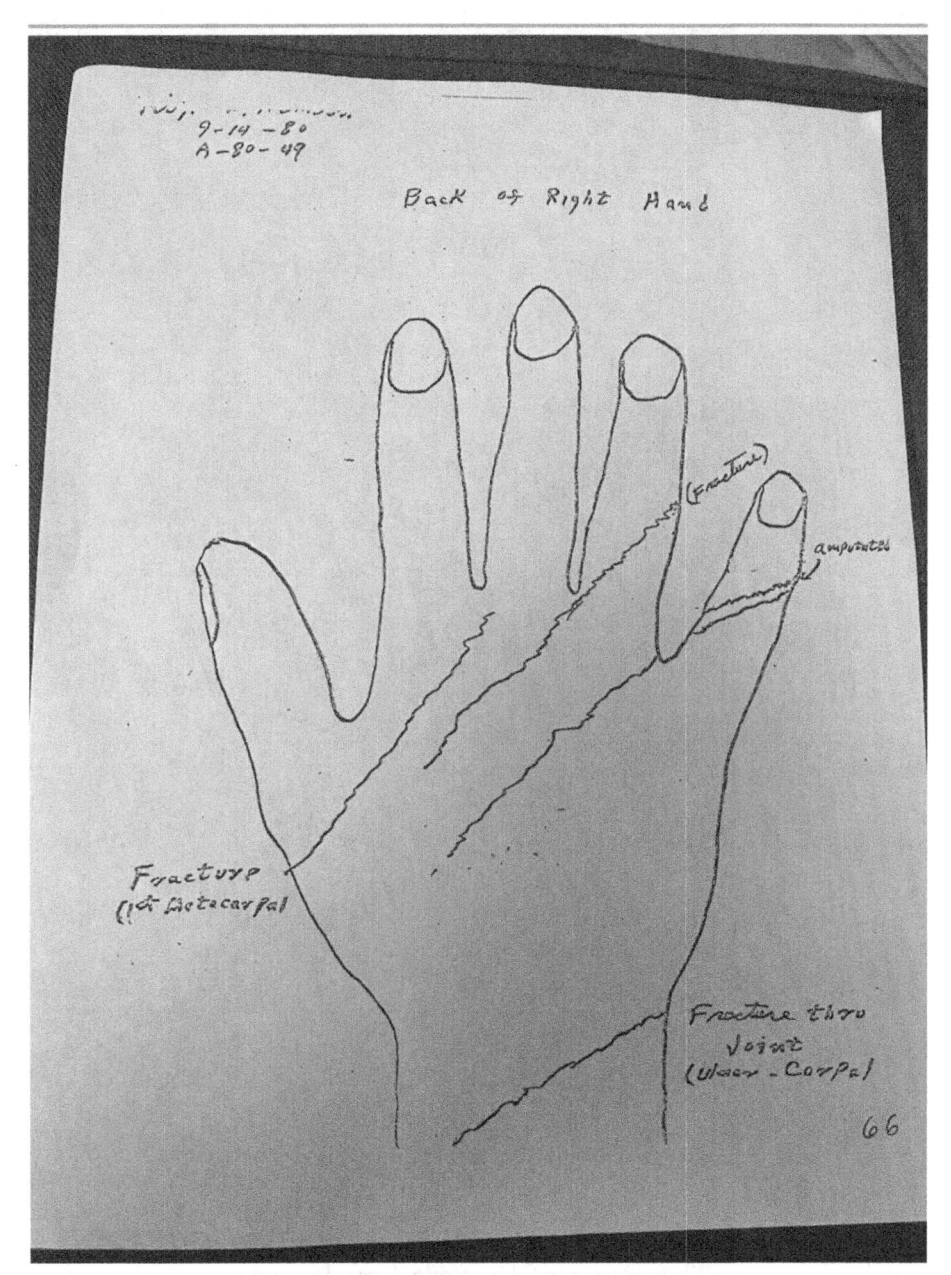

Axed!

The Back of Roger's Right Hand

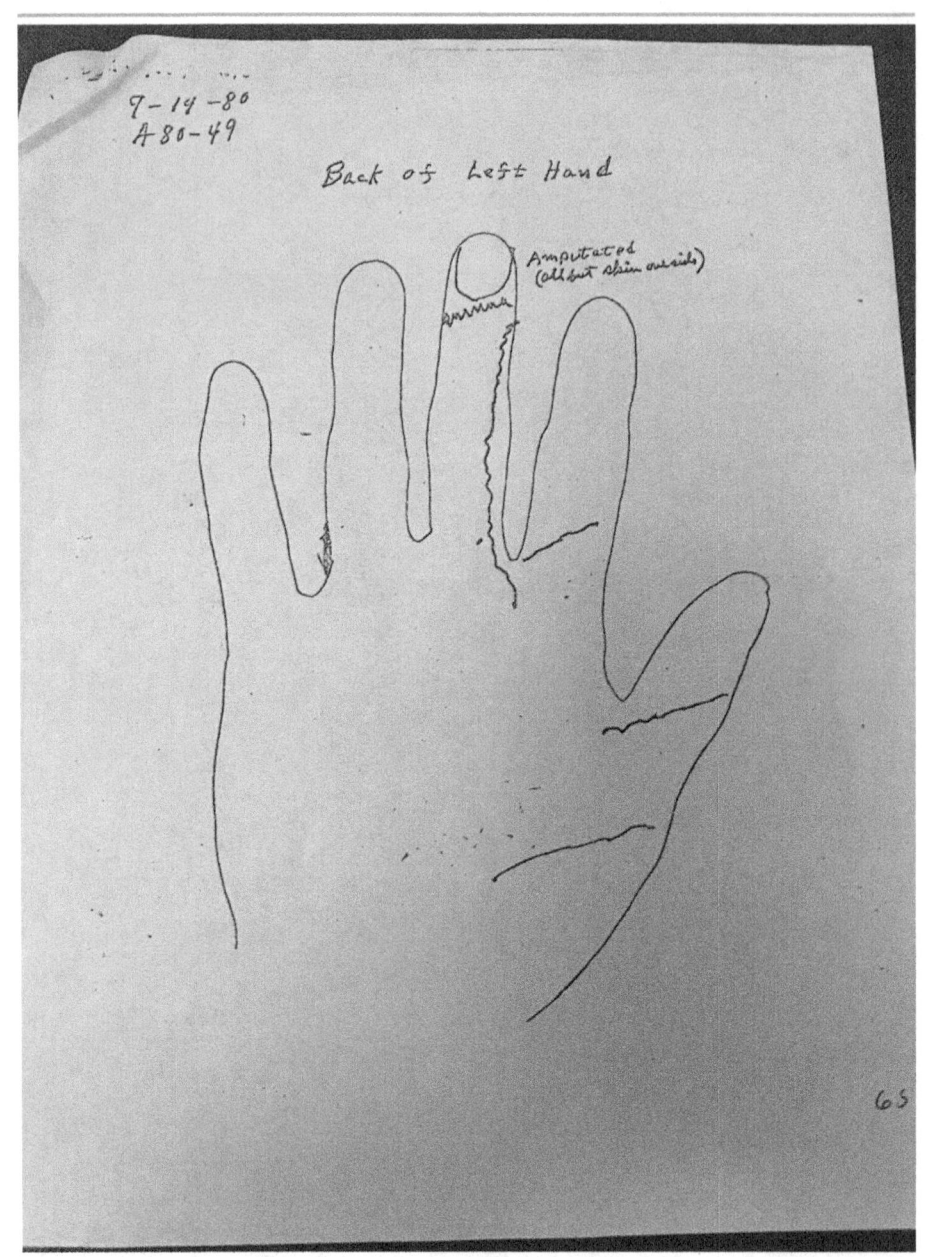

The Back of Roger's Left Hand

Axed!

Rose's death certificate states multiple causes of death: acute blood loss, brain injuries, multiple lacerations to the scalp and skull, a brain laceration, a brain contusion, subarachnoid hemorrhaging, and multiple penetrating wounds to posterior head. Injury occurred due to multiple penetrating wounds to posterior head. Approximate interval between onset and death was 2-5 minutes.

Roger's death certificate also states multiple causes of death: acute blood loss, brain injuries, multiple lacerations to the scalp, skull, and brain and subarachnoid hemorrhaging; and multiple penetrating wounds to posterior head. Approximate interval between onset and death for him was also 2-5 minutes. There were no signs of sexual abuse on either victim.

It appeared their suitcases were rifled through, and Roger's billfold meticulously gone through with the contents thrown on the floor and money taken from it. A photo of one of Roger's nieces from his billfold was torn up and thrown on the floor. Rose's billfold did not appear to be gone through and was found lying on the side of the bed she lay on. Oddly Roger's eyeglasses were lying by her billfold on her side of the bed.

Even though money was taken from Roger's billfold, the feeling of law enforcement is that this crime was not for the purpose of robbery. They feel it is more of a personal nature since the murders were so gruesome, violent, and "overkill."

"In 1992, Iowa County Sheriff James Slockett told Cedar Rapids Gazette reporters Rick Smith and Jeff Burnham that he was convinced the murders were driven by 'revenge,' a motive that explains the personal nature of the vicious attacks."

I compare the experience of a loved one being murdered to a big gaping wound. The physician sews it up, and then you wait for it to heal. It starts the healing process, and then something comes along to bump it, causing pain or, perhaps even worse, opening it up again to the extent to where it bleeds. The physician may need to sew it up again, and the healing process starts all over again. But the good news is that over the years, my wound from this tragedy has not bled as much or taken as long to heal. The wound scar, however, is always there. God again has been faithful to be there with me every step of the way. He has helped my wound to heal and enabled me to carry on down this less-traveled road.

The poem "Footprints" by Mary Stevenson describes how I felt at the time. She talks about walking on the beach with the Lord and how scenes from her life flash before her. From all of the scenes, she notices two sets of footprints, hers and the Lord's. But when she got to the last scene, she only noticed one set of footprints. This really disturbed her, so she questioned the Lord why, in her greatest time of need in life, the saddest and lowest part of her life, he had deserted her. The Lord replied that he loved her very much, and it was at these times he carried her. This resulted in only one set of footprints, his.

There were times that God carried me after Roger's murder when I was too weak to walk down my less-traveled road by myself and on my own power.

Chapter 7

A New Life

Scripture: Now faith is the assurance of things hoped for, the conviction of things not seen.
—Hebrews 11:1.

In an earlier chapter, I lamented how I did not want to remain single for the rest of my life. Well, God honored that desire of my heart. I immersed myself in my home church, King Hill Baptist. And low and behold, we formed a single's group of divorced, widowed, and widowers. Our singles group was very active and grew into a sizable group. It was in that group that I became acquainted with my present husband, Vernie. We officially began dating in October of 1981. The singles group quickly dwindled over a six-month time span to just a few members. Couples married in November of 1981, January of 1982, we married in February 1982, and the final couple in June of 1982.

Vernie and I were married on February 12 at King Hill Baptist church in St. Joseph, Missouri, and have celebrated over 40 years of marriage. Our honeymoon was hurried as I was in my final classes in college for my teaching degree and doing my student teaching at the grade school I attended as a child, Hyde Elementary.

After our wedding, Vernie and I continued to live in the two-story house that Roger and I had bought. In May of 1982, Vernie's youngest daughter by his first wife came to visit and decided to stay and live with us. She was 16 at the time and lived with us for a year before returning to live with her mother in Washington state. Vernie had four daughters by his first wife, with this daughter being the youngest of the four. So, he certainly was no stranger to children, especially girls.

One time on a bowling date, Vernie had stated that he wouldn't take a million for his girls, but he wouldn't want to give a dime for another one. He had to eventually eat his words on that one. Vernie knew that having a child was very important to me, so we pursued trying to have a child of our own. But as with Roger, my body was not cooperating in that department. So, we also decided to try the adoption route. The problem we faced was that we had not been married the preferred five years, and if we waited the five years, Vernie would be considered too old to adopt since he would then be 49 at the end of that time span. We applied to an adoption agency in Georgia but found out they were not reputable.

Then we applied for a foreign adoption from an agency out of Olathe, Kansas, for a Samoan child. Vernie was not happy with the thought of adopting a male child who could possibly have major health problems. About the time all this was going on, I learned of an infertility seminar being held at a home for unwed mothers in Kansas City, Missouri, called The Lighthouse. A speaker at the seminar was an attorney who told of the anguish of his and his wife's infertility issues. After the meeting, I confided to the attorney Vernie and my infertility issues and asked him if he ever did private adoptions. He said he did, and he told us that he might have a situation coming up soon and to send him our information. I thought it was big talk, just like

Axed!

the rest of those adoption people. About a month later, the attorney called to ask if we were still interested in a baby. *Were we still interested?* I about fell over. Yes, we were still interested in a baby! The birth mother had gone into false labor earlier, but she was again at the hospital and was apparently going to deliver this time. It was a little of a Deja Vue situation because, again, I found myself fervently petitioning God that the birth mother carry through with giving the baby up for adoption. While in the midst of all of this, I felt God gave me the scripture from Hebrews that I quoted at the beginning of this chapter. I felt it was God reassuring me that everything was going to work out this time. And it did!

Our wonderful baby girl was born in August, and we named her Corey Lynn. Cora was the name of Vernie's mom, so Corey was a version of that, and Lynn was my middle name. Now that prayer that the big, old two-story house that I wanted a child in had been granted to me. Within three years, I became doubly blessed by two miracles from God. Not only had God blessed me with a godly, Christian husband, but now a beautiful baby girl.

Earlier, I stated Vernie would have to eat his words about not giving a penny for another child. Since Corey's adoption was private through an attorney, we spent thousands of dollars on her adoption with attorney fees, home study fees, and social worker fees. It was a situation I could kid Vernie about years later.

Corey knew from the time she was young that she was adopted. And she also knew she had been prayed for and given to us as a gift from God. But the fact that she was adopted seemed to always weigh heavy on her because she knew for us to adopt her, someone had to give her up. And what was the reason she was given up by her birth mom? I tried to give her reasons I knew of as to why she would have been relinquished for adoption and to reassure her she was prayed for and very much wanted, but it was in vain.

When Corey became old enough, she searched and found her biological birth mother and grandmother. She visited them a couple of times and even took me on the last visit. The birth mother thanked me for raising Corey, and I am thankful Corey shared this experience with me. Corey was glad in one respect that she had found them and had her curiosity satisfied, but on the other hand, she wished she had left it alone. You just can't turn back the hands of time after over 25 years!

After Corey got old enough to be in Middle School, I felt it was time to start my teaching career. I interviewed for a third-grade position at North Andrew RVI in Rosendale, Missouri. It was a reasonably new school that housed kindergarten through 12th grade in the country about 15 miles north of where I lived. The interviewing principal asked me if I would consider taking the Special Education teaching position of kindergarten through fourth grade. If I did, the school would pay my college fees to return to school to get certified in Special Education. My attitude was *sure, why not?* I had no idea what I was getting myself into, but God knew exactly where I needed to be. I am thankful that God gave me 17 years of teaching Special Ed students at North Andrew, and I retired in May of 2016.

Corey's first marriage failed, but she married again, and God blessed me again with three beautiful granddaughters through Corey: Ava Lynn, Tracy Alivia, and Addison Rose. Yes, I have a granddaughter with the middle name Rose. When Corey had Ava, she wanted to give her the middle name of Rose because she liked it. But I asked her not to do that because the name Rose had a negative connotation for me. But as time passed and I had healed more from the murder, I told Corey that the name Rose would be a good name for Addison because we could then call her Addy Rose, and then *Rose* would then have a positive meaning for me.

My life has not been without physical problems and pain. I was adding up the surgeries I have had throughout my 70 years. I have had: torn ligaments in my left knee, my left ovary and tube removed and later a total hysterectomy, part of my colon removed, six back surgeries including fusions of my lower back, three neck surgeries with one being a fusion, part of thyroid removed, total replacements of both shoulders, two heart stint surgeries, cataract surgery in both eyes, carpal tunnel surgeries on both wrists, tendinitis surgery on my left wrist, tonsils removed, wisdom teeth extracted, and a total left knee replacement. That is a lot of surgeries God has brought me through.

My beloved mom passed in May 2019, three days after my 67th birthday. We found out she had Non- Hodgins Lymphoma in February, and after her third chemo treatment in May, she passed on the 29th. She was my sounding board throughout dealing with Roger's death and one of my best friends. She is sorely missed.

During Vernie and my 40 years together, we accomplished many things. We have built two new houses together while putting a lot of our own sweat and muscle into them. During COVID, we moved to Texas to a Senior Community to be closer to Corey and the granddaughters. I loved being a mother, and I now love being *Grandma*.

God has taken me through many life twists and turns on this road into a new life, for which I thank and praise him. But the murder of Roger has hung over my head all these years. An article that appeared on the internet website of Iowa unsolved murders, states, "By the 1990's his (Roger's) wife Marcella, with whom he had no children, had remarried and moved on with her life." Remarried and moved on, I think that is what God wanted me to do, but that is not to say that the murder of Roger was ever forgotten. It has always been with me, that ever-present healed-over sore I described earlier.

Time has a way of healing things for us with God's help. The road I chose back in 1970 has taken me on many twists and turns into a new life.

Chapter 8

Harassment

Scripture: For if you forgive others their trespasses, your heavenly Father will also forgive you, but if you do not forgive others their trespasses, neither will your Father forgive your trespasses.
—Matthew 6: 14-15.

There are several scriptures in the Bible about forgiveness. It is not an option for us; we do not have a choice to forgive or not. We are commanded by God to do it.

On March 21, 2016, I received a friend request on Facebook from someone I did not know, and along with it came the following message: *"You know you and your husband will go to hell for killing your ex-husband and Rose, right?"*

I was obviously shaken by this message for several reasons. Not knowing who the person was and his or her connection, if any, to the crime. Why had he or she waited so long, 36 years later, to write such a horrible accusation to me? I had nothing to do with the crime. Furthermore, why was my husband Vernie accused of such a thing when we didn't even start dating until October 1981? He wasn't even in the picture, so to speak, back in 1980. Nonetheless, it was disturbing to think someone out there was fixating on the crime after all these years and was lashing out at me, who was also a victim of the crime. I just happened to be still alive.

I blocked the person on Facebook so I would not get any more messages from them, and I definitely did not respond to their message.

Then over a year later, on May 23, 2017, I started receiving emails from an email address listed as roseburkert80@yahoo.com. Rose was the girl killed with Roger, and 1980 was the year they were murdered.

The first email said the following:

Subject: We haven't met
Hi Marcella!
I think it's time that you and I finally meet. Am I angry?
Sure I am. You sent your father and his psycho brother to murder me. I know the plan was to take care of the husband, but why me? I don't understand how you sleep at night knowing that you took my life and protected those who played a part in it. Aren't you a Christian? You DO get that no amount of Bible-reading will stop you from going to Hell for what you've done to me. You can tell yourself you're not a murderer if you want. You can tell yourself that you've made up for it in other ways, but you took two lives. YOU did....and then you profited. There's no doubt you'll burn in Hell forever for that.

It looks like those two disgusting pigs have died (referring to my dad and Uncle Charles). Hey, we all do, whether brutally or peacefully in our sleep. It's after death that really matters, though, and you're in for a lot of hellfire. I'm sorry we didn't get to meet face to face, other than when you came to my funeral, looked at me, and walked away. I doubt my face haunts your dreams, but I hope so. If not, it really should, but I wouldn't expect that from a cold-hearted murderous bitch.

Know this: There are things in motion, and they will prove what you've done. You certainly haven't deserved your freedom the last 37 years—especially with the money you made for being a murderer, but your time is closing in, and even if we don't manage to see you locked up in this lifetime, we'll know you couldn't escape God's judgment. Everyone gets what they deserve in the end. You're an awful human being ... a monster. You took someone's mother ... you took a life. You'll pay for it one way or another. But trust me when I tell you I believe I have the final nail that will pin you to mine and Roger's death.

Think of my face when you go to sleep. You don't deserve peace.

Rose

Was it a coincidence that this was a couple of days after Rose's birthday on May 21?

On May 30, here came another one. It said the following:
Subject: You don't want to confront this?
"Hey, murderer! Have you convinced yourself that you've prayed away any chance you'll burn in Hell? Sorry, but it doesn't work that way. If you helped to cover up a crime, and friends and family never got answers because you couldn't take responsibility, then your prayers are pointless. You're going to burn in Hell with your father and uncle for eternity. You're a fat ugly disgrace of a human being, allowing such a brutal thing to happen to me and Roger.

You're a sick twisted freak. I'm going to make sure everyone knows you, knows the truth. I hope you're ready to start answering questions.

—Rose"

That email came on Roger's birthday.

Another one came on June 1:

"Have you thought about telling the truth yet? You're getting up there in years. Are you sure you want to burn in Hell for eternity?"

And then a final one came on June 6:

Subject: Do you sleep?

"I was wondering if you think about my brutal murder often.

I know you go to church weekly. Your husband even ushers. Do you believe that there's some amount of favor you can build with God to work your way out of Hell?

I don't think so, Marcella. You prompted a brutal double-murder and hid it for 36 years. The very fact that you stay silent is what will one day guarantee your passage into Hell. You can go to church weekly, but God will never forgive you for lying and benefitting off the brutal crime you've helped commit.

Your father is undoubtedly burning in Hell, and you'll be next."

The last two were NOT signed "Rose."

These emails were very upsetting to me. If the author of them was trying to get my mind working overtime, she/he had succeeded.

Axed!

I decided to alert my local sheriff's office of this situation to see what could be done about it. I was told that the emails fell under the umbrella of CyberCrime. Those types of crimes were handled by our Missouri Highway Patrol out of Lee Summit, Missouri. I was assured by the Andrew County Sheriff's Office that my case would be forwarded to the highway patrol, who would handle the case.

I believe it was a week later when I called the Andrew County Sheriff's Office to find out about my case. Nothing had been done about it. So being the determined person that I am, I took it upon myself to contact the highway patrol. I spoke with a sergeant who was very helpful. I forwarded copies of the emails to him. I later learned that a court order had to be issued by the court to subpoena *Yahoo!* to find out the true sender of the emails, which took months.

Finally, the results came in, and he asked me if I knew anyone in the Des Moines, Iowa area. I told him I didn't personally know the sender of the Facebook message back in March of 2016, but from checking his information out on his Facebook profile, he was from that area. The Sergeant confirmed my suspicions that it was indeed the same person.

The case was sent from Missouri to Iowa County Sheriff's office because the writer of the emails lived in Iowa, and the emailer had referenced an unsolved murder in his emails. The Iowa Sheriff's deputy contacted the emailer and stated he was very remorseful for what he had done. He was willing to apologize over the phone, in a letter, or however I wanted. So, I was asked if I wanted to pursue legal action against the man.

I pondered the situation and eventually came up with the belief that he should be prosecuted. The man had cyberbullied me. When I taught school for 17 years, we teachers worked hard at a no tolerance of bullying among students. Now why should an adult man get away with it? I did not hold any animosity toward the young man and forgave him for his actions, but we, as Christians, when we sin and disobey God, pay the consequences for our actions. Yet God forgives us. So even though I had forgiven this man, he still should reap consequences from the law and hopefully not do it again to anyone else.

The Sheriff's Office was to contact the Polk County Prosecutor's office to have the offender prosecuted. I eventually got an email from the sheriff stating he could not find a prosecutor in the Polk County office that would take the case.

What, I thought? Does the Prosecutor's Office choose what crimes they prosecute when a person breaks the law? True, this crime was not a rape or murder, but this guy had invaded my mind and personal space and had inflicted mental distress on me for days, if not months. And as I look at it, breaking the law is breaking the law, whether it be a little or big crime.

Again, being the determined person I am, I called the Polk County Iowa Prosecutor's Office to ask how they could pick and choose who to prosecute that violates the law. A lady answered the phone and asked for the prosecutor's name that would not take the case, and she said that was not the usual way they conducted their office. After visiting with the Iowa County Sheriff again, it was discovered he had not talked to the Prosecutor's Office but the police department. I asked the sheriff to contact the Prosecutor's

Office to give them the case information, but again a few days later, I followed up to make sure my request had been accomplished. My point in telling this part of my story is to encourage the readers that you are your own best advocate. Follow up, call, call, and call again. And don't take "no" for an answer until you have exhausted every avenue. Our law offices are overworked at best, and the "squeaky wheel gets the oil" theory seems to apply in this case.

I must brag on the Iowa Polk County Prosecutor's office. Within a day, I was contacted by a paralegal in that office. She was a very kind and compassionate woman who assured me that her office would certainly advocate for me to try and get some justice for me on the email harassment issue. She offered her assistance for any issues or questions I might have and said not to hesitate to call her.

My harassment case was handled within a few weeks. The harasser was arrested and kept in jail overnight. His trial was held on April 10, 2018, and he pled guilty to all four harassment charges. Count 1: Harassment in the Third Degree in violation of Iowa Code section(s) 708.7 (4). Count II: Harassment in the Third Degree in violation of Iowa Code Section(s) 708.7(4). Count III: Harassment in the Third Degree in violation of Iowa Code Section(s) 708.7 (4). Count IV: Harassment in the Third Degree in violation of Iowa Code Section(s) 708.7 (4).

The Iowa District Court for Polk County adjudged the defendant guilty of four counts of Harassment in the third degree in violation of Iowa Code Sections (s) 708.7 (4). He was ordered by the court to pay a total of $400 for the four charges, to pay for, cooperate with and complete a Mental Health Evaluation within 30 days of the court order, and to complete any recommended treatment/education and aftercare. He was placed on 12 months' probation to be supervised by the Department of Correctional Services. There was a court-ordered protection on me from him for the following five years, remaining in effect through 04/10/2023. I was told Polk County would issue another restraining order on him if, at the end of those five years, he harassed me again.

Also, if I chose to participate in what Iowa calls a VORP meeting, the man would be so ordered. This was a supervised face-to-face meeting with him for me to ask him any questions I might have, and he any questions of me. I wasn't sure if I wanted to meet him and was advised by several friends to not do the meeting. But I hoped meeting him would be a good witness to him, and perhaps I could get some questions answered. He also was ordered to pay me restitution for my mileage to Iowa, my meals, and my motel while there for the meeting.

The meeting was held at the Prosecuting Attorney's Office with a hired mediator and the prosecutor's assistant present. I was allowed to have two people present for moral support. My cousin accompanied me to Iowa to give me that support.

The mediator met with me first to let me know how the meeting would unfold. When the harasser arrived, the mediator met with him to make sure there didn't seem to be any anger that would erupt. After he was brought in to meet me, he spoke first. He thanked me for coming and apologized for his actions. He expressed embarrassment and shame for his actions, that what he had done to me was cruel and not at all reflective of the person he wanted to be. He was tearful at times and said he had time to consider how his decisions had impacted me. I felt, as well

Axed!

as the prosecutor's assistant and the mediator, that he was being truly remorseful and just not acting. I thanked the harasser for coming, and I told him about my faith, that I had forgiven him, and I was sure that God had as well. I read the following letter to him:

Dear Mr. _____,

I pray you are interested in the things I am about to explain to you. Perhaps you will better understand the impact of your actions after listening.

In September of 1980, almost 38 years ago, I lost my first husband, Roger Atkison, to a brutal murder. When it happened, I lost my husband of 7 years, my teenage sweetheart of 13 years (I dated Roger since I was 15 ½ years old), my provider since he was the only one employed full time, my hopes of a family, and who I believed was my soul mate. At the time I was dealing with all of this loss, I was also coming to terms with the fact that I had been betrayed by Roger and his adulterous relationship with Rose. God's holy word makes it perfectly clear that adultery is sin. Out of their two murders came two dead victims, but also out of those two murders came many living victims, me being one. My God has been with me throughout this whole process and has gotten me through when I could not go any further on my own. Over the years, I have tried not to emphasize the role of being a living victim. However, when someone comes along like yourself and makes such horrible accusations, I feel like I am victimized all over again. When you are a living victim of a crime, especially so horrific, it never ever leaves you. By the grace of God, I have survived.

Within a little over a year after Roger's death, God provided me with a wonderful husband, and three years later, he provided us with a beautiful, adopted baby girl. God has truly blessed me over the years.

To this day, I would love to see the murders solved. This situation has been an albatross around my neck for almost 38 years. Like you said in one of your emails, I am not getting any younger. I have hoped and prayed it would be solved before I die. I have tried to notify the Iowa DCI or Sheriff's Office any time I have learned anything that could be of help in solving this case.

You accused my father of being the perpetrator and stated he was burning in Hell. I had just lost my father in February of 2017, and for a long time, I had prayed for his salvation. Shortly before his death, he indicated to me that he was saved. Without God's wonderful saving grace, your comments regarding my dad burning in Hell would have been quite unbearable. They were not pleasant as it was and created more unnecessary trauma in my life.

You look like a nice young man, and I pray that you will never subject your life again to the problem this has caused you. I hope and pray this will provide you with a learning experience that will guide you in the right direction for the rest of your life.

I have been praying for you.

I found out that this man had stumbled across the murder case on Iowa's Cold Cases on the internet approximately three years earlier. He had felt it should have been solved and began obsessing about it. He indicated he had found my email address and things about me from the internet. This young man was not even born until April of 1981, so he was not even alive when the murders occurred.

Axed!

After reading the letter to him, he stated how he had talked to a detective from the murder case who shot down his ideas about the crime. This made him feel horrible about what he had done to me. He apologized again and told me he would never be a problem for me in the future. I told him I did not want him to obsess about his actions but rather to learn from them, move forward, and be a better person for it. At the end of the meeting, I asked if I could hug him, and he agreed. As we hugged, he sobbed, and I told him not to let this experience define him.

Later the prosecutor's assistant said I had given him the best gift that he could have received through this horrible ordeal which was forgiveness. I had explained earlier to him that God forgives, and we are commanded to forgive. We are not given a choice.

I left the meeting that day, glad that I had taken a risk and attended the meeting. I had a couple of friends who had cautioned me that it didn't sound like a good idea, maybe even dangerous. But I feel it is what God wanted me to do.

I am grateful to the Iowa Polk County office and staff for allowing the meeting to take place and for the harasser being strong enough to face me and apologize. It took a mighty big man to face me and to apologize to me, so if you ever read this book, thank you again. I gained healing from this experience and hope you did too.

The road less traveled has granted me some unexpected hurt and **healing**.

Chapter 9

The Elephant in the Room

Scripture: "Blessed is the man who preserves under trial, because when he has stood the test, he will receive the crown of life that God has promised to those who love him."

—James1:12

The proverbial saying is, "Everyone is ignoring the elephant in the room." In other words, the elephant is in the middle of the room where no one can ignore it, it is obvious, but ... no one wants to talk about it. I guess the feeling is to *just ignore it, and it will go away.*

But the elephant is s-o-o-o big and obvious, it can't be ignored.

The obvious elephant in the room for me is the suspicion by many that my father had something to do with Roger's death, whether hiring it done or doing it himself. Since Dad's brother, Charles, was a serial killer, he also was a suspect.

From the very beginning of Roger's death, I thought my dad had acted strangely, but in such cases of death by murder like Roger's, people will act strangely. I remember that when Dad, Mom, and I went to view Roger's body for the first time at Rupp's Funeral Home, Dad told me, "Now, when you see Roger's body, don't cry." And I didn't. I thought this was a very odd request since anyone would expect a wife to cry under the circumstances. The thought had crossed my mind that he had something to do with the murder, but I didn't want to think that my dad could be capable of such a horrific thing. Besides, I thought, "How in the world could my dad ever think he was doing me a favor by murdering Roger?"

Another factor I thought played into this whole situation was that Dad had many affairs on Mom. "Why would Dad think it okay for him and not Roger? Could he have believed it okay for himself but not okay for his son-in-law?" I do know that when Vernie, my present husband, went to marry me, Dad told him, "You had better not ever hurt Marcella." That statement from Dad seemed odd, yet not odd if you take it in the context of his daughter, me, being terribly hurt by my first husband, Roger.

There have been rumors that Dad hired some people to do the killing. Various people he could have hired have been questioned by law enforcement. I have heard that three of those people could have been someone that worked for him at the moving business and/or his brother Charles. I think if Dad had wanted something like that done, I think he would have taken care of it himself. Besides, what did he have against Rose? To my knowledge, he didn't know her, nor had he ever met her. There surely were opportunities that he could have done the killing of just Roger without involving Rose too. If he had known she had a small child, I think that would have been another reason for him not to have killed her.

There have been other rumors of Dad sitting in a bar and talking about killing Roger, but that is what they are—rumors. No one has stepped forward to verify that rumor or various other rumors to law enforcement.

Before my dad died, I asked him several times about Roger's murder, but he never indicated to me that he had anything to do with it. I alerted the chaplain of Hospice to the situation of Roger's murder in case there was a reason Dad needed to make a confession before death. But there never was a confession forthcoming to my knowledge.

My dad, as well as many of us, was fingerprinted, given a lie detector test, and thoroughly questioned regarding the murders. Our DNA did not match up with the DNA on file from the bloody towel that was found in the motel bathroom from the crime scene.

I believe had facts come out back in 1980 when Roger was murdered that my dad could have had something to do with it or orchestrated the murders, it would have been hard to have processed that information along with everything else at that time. But now I just want to know no matter how painful it might be.

Another family suspect was my dad's youngest brother, Charles Hatcher. Charles was a serial killer that was roaming the streets at the time Roger was killed. I learned that a man was being held on a child abduction/murder charge in St. Joseph by the police department. That man was going by the name of Richard Clark, but when I learned his real name was Charles Hatcher, I called the St. Joseph Police Department and asked that Charles be questioned if he had anything to do with Roger's murder. He was questioned and denied anything to do with Roger and Rose's murder. He was known to not be in the immediate area of the deaths. And he was living on the streets without any known means of transportation. He was purported to be working at a Taco Tico in another part of Iowa, while his timecard showed him to be working at the time frame of the crime. Another factor was that Charles usually molested and then killed young boys. Serial killers usually have a pattern to their killing, and Roger and Rose's murder did not match his pattern of killing.

Can you imagine living for over 40 years with all my unanswered questions AND wondering all those years if my dad could have had anything to do with it? Wondering if there had been a big family cover-up of facts just because they thought they were doing me a favor? Thinking it was better I didn't know the truth? Little did they know not knowing the truth all these years has been just about as painful as having known the truth and being able to put closure on this tragedy. Or wondering if the perpetrator was a friend or relative on Roger's side, and what in the world was the motive?

So regardless of who the murderer(s) were, now that I am old, I just want to know who did it and why and put closure to that whole part of my past. I long for that closure. "God, if you see fit, please give me that closure. Amen."

The less traveled road with this elephant in the room has had many bumps, twists, and turns. But God was there to help me through all of them.

Chapter 10

Person(s) of Interest?

Scripture: "And you shall know the truth, and the truth shall set you free."
—John 8:32

    This case is so complex that when you take the possible list of person(s) of interest, it becomes overwhelming at best. In this chapter, I will not use the person's real name.

Person #1: Rose's jilted boyfriend, David. Not too long before Roger entered Rose's life, she had thrown out her boyfriend, supposedly because of his drug use. David did not take to the separation kindly, and according to Rose, he harassed and stalked her. Rumors were going around that Rose suspected her ex-boyfriend of killing her dog and hanging it in a tree in her front yard. However, the fact is that the dog was found dead at the end of the neighbor's driveway, apparently hit by a car. She had gone to her local law enforcement agency, the Andrew County Sheriff's Office, not too long before her murder and stated if anything happened to her, look at her ex-boyfriend, David.

    David was to have been given a lie detector test and passed. He also was to have had a solid alibi, which was being at his job working the night shift the Friday night/Saturday morning of the murders.

    Question: Could he have had a friend willing to commit murder for him, or could he have hired someone?

Axed!

Person(s) #2: One or more of the GTE employees. The relationship between Roger and Rose was common knowledge among his fellow workers. It is rumored that some of the men were having affairs on their wives and possibly even knew Rose quite well. Could one of them have approached Rose for an affair, and she rebuffed him to be with Roger, thus insulting his male ego?

His fellow home base GTE workers in Savannah, Missouri, knew where he was that week in Kahoka. Two fellow employees, Matt and Greg who also knew that Rose was with Roger in Kahoka and of Roger's plans to take her to the Amanas for the weekend.

"...(Matt) advised the reporting agent that he was present during the telephone conversation between his supervisor and (Roger) and overheard his supervisor advise Roger not to use a company-paid motel for his affair. He stated he was sitting in his supervisor's office when he contacted (Roger).

When asked by the reporting agent why (Roger) would have been in Iowa, he stated that he knew why Roger was in Iowa—because he was in the office of their supervisor at about 4:45 PM on Thursday, September 4, 1980, when he overheard a telephone conversation between the supervisor and him. The supervisor advised Atkison to go up to this German community in Iowa and use a motel there." *

*Quoted material taken from (Matt's) interview case no. 80006274 on 9/14/80 exhibit #10-13.

Telephone employees many times carried a machete to hack undergrowth around telephone poles which is an instrument comparable to the weapon speculated in killing the couple.

On Saturday, September 13, my mother made a phone call to Roger's brother's house late that afternoon to inform his family of his death. Matt answered his brother's phone, and my mother made one of two statements, "Roger has been found dead," or "Roger has been found dead with another woman." Whichever statement she made to him, he replied, "I know." Since the family was just being told about the murders, how did he know this information? Another strange thing about this is that Matt did not go ahead and tell the other family members about the murders. The family did not learn about it until they returned from their town celebration, and the local sheriff was waiting to tell them the news.

Then there is another strange incident related to Matt and Greg that had to do with my Vega that Roger drove to work the morning he left for Kahoka. I go into depth about this incident in Chapter 10 titled The Mystery of the Vega.

Law enforcement wanted a relative to go to Iowa to identify the body. My mom was adamant that it would not be me that would do it, so Roger's brother said he would. He wanted his wife to go with him, but Matt was insistent on going, so he and Roger's brother went together. On the way to the morgue, the two men stopped by the Holiday Inn, where the investigation was still being conducted. Before going up to the room where the murder took place, Matt pulled his car around to a motel dumpster and said he needed to get rid of some rotten watermelon in his car trunk. After that, at the room, Matt told the investigators that he needed Roger's company key ring to take back to the Savannah office. Instead of the key ring being held as evidence, it was turned over to Matt. Questions are raised in my mind as to what was so important on that key ring that it had to be acquired by Matt before the crime scene investigation had been completed. And why did the

Axed!

investigators allow the key ring, which was part of a crime scene, to be taken by Matt?

Once at the morgue, Roger's brother had to identify Roger's body by himself because Matt said he couldn't do it, even after he insisted that the brother's wife stay home, and he be the one to accompany him to accomplish the task.

Person #3: The spouse, which is me. Statistics show that it is usually someone close to the victim when it appears to have a lot of "overkill," and usually, the spouse is the first one that is suspected. I willingly got fingerprinted, took a lie detector test, and cooperated with law enforcement.

Here are the questions asked of me on the lie detector test:

---Do you know if the word_____was on the motel door/walls?
1. Murder
2. Kill
3. That
4. No
5. Please
6. Help
7. This

---Do they call you Marcie?
---Do you intend to answer questions truthfully?
---Did you kill Roger and/or Rose?
---Did you plan the murders of Roger and/or Rose?
---Are you afraid I'll ask you any questions you haven't already been told about?
---Do you know who killed Roger and/or Rose other than what we've talked about?

---In the past five years, have you ever hurt anyone?
---Have you had drugs in the last 8 hours?
---Have you answered all the questions truthfully?

My alibi was I had been babysitting the Black's daughter since Saturday, September 6, 1980. There were also two college-age brothers present during the stay at the Black home, one that had been home sick that week. I did know that Roger was going to Kahoka but did not know he was going to Iowa. And I did not know about Rose or any other affairs that Roger might have had during our marriage.

A newspaper article states, "Slockett (the sheriff at the time of the murders) said Marcie Atkison has been eliminated as a suspect."

Person(s) #4: My dad and uncle. I tell about them in the chapter titled, Elephant in the Room.

Person #5: The motel bartender. There was a rumor that Roger or Rose argued with the motel bartender. He supposedly disappeared without his paycheck, abandoned his truck in Iowa City 22 miles east of the crime, and abruptly enlisted in the military and was sent to Germany. But the rumor of an argument was checked out to be false. There was the story that the bartender was living in the parking lot in his truck at the motel at the time of the crime. Could he have seen the killer/killers leaving, and could he identify them? Could that be why he ran? Or was he afraid his lifestyle would make him suspect?

"He never did pick up his last paycheck, which looked suspicious, but he satisfied us that it was for personal reasons not connected to the crime," Slockett stated. "He was questioned when he returned to the United States." In the newspaper article "Prime Suspect Knew Victim," the sheriff states, "One man was eliminated as a suspect after taking a lie detector test nine times. The individual was a bartender at the Amana Holiday Inn, and he moved south after the killings. He joined the Army and was sent to Germany." *

I have to ask, *What? You gave the man nine tries to clear himself? How many honest people need to take nine lie detector tests to finally pass?*

Scenario #6: A man named Raymundo Esparza is believed to have committed a similar crime in Galesburg, Illinois, in June of 1980 at the Sheraton Inn. The victim was a 25-year-old Peoria, Illinois, salesman named William R. Kyle Jr. There are several similarities between the two crimes. The one significant discrepancy was the Galesburg murder had sexual overtones. Esparza was believed to have been in Iowa City the night of the Amana deaths. I explore this more in "The Rest of the Story" chapter.

Scenario #7: Someone randomly wandered off Interstate 80 looking for someone to kill.

Scenario #8: An obsessed farmhand that Rose had earlier claimed had broken into her house prior to the murders was thought to be 12 miles due north of the Holiday Inn at the time of the murders.

Scenario #9: There had been recent cattle mutilations in Iowa; could their murders be the next step to human sacrifice?

Scenario #10: A jealous husband from Roger's affair with his wife. There have been rumors that Roger had affairs with other women. Could one of them have gotten revenge for the affair?

Scenario #11: Another person that law enforcement interviewed was a relative of Rose. He was considered a person of interest due to his being in the Iowa area at the time they were killed. The story has come out that the relative told a friend that he was going over to the Amana Colonies to see a family member. There was some speculation that the relative may not have been happy with the way Rose was raising her daughter, and he and his wife at the time could not have children, so that could have been the motive.

Scenario #12: At the time of the murders, the motel was completely occupied with a Mortician's Convention. The question has been asked, "Could one or more of the morticians have wanted to kill to see what it felt like? Could one or more of them have desired to see what it was like to be on the other end of the death process by killing the couple?"

After reading the list of persons of interest, the reader needs to keep in mind these key elements of the crime:

1) The killer/killers needed to know where Roger and Rose were staying (Kahoka).

2) They needed to know where they were going (Amana Colonies).

3) They needed an idea of when they would be headed to the Amanas (after Roger got off work).

4) Possibly what vehicle they would be driving (Rose's car), and to possibly follow them while driving without being detected.

Who were the people that would have knowledge of those factors?

In the *Des Moines Register*, a staff writer by the name of Nick Lamberto reported, "After 51 months of patient

Axed!

probing, Iowa County Sheriff James Slockett said Monday he is now 99 percent sure he knows who committed the double murders at the Amana Holiday Inn on Interstate 80 east of Williamsburg. 'Everything points to one individual,' Slockett said. 'By a process of elimination, we have narrowed it down to one suspect, and that person has been a suspect for a long time. I say I'm 99 percent sure the person did it or was part of the double homicide.' But proving his prime suspect is guilty is another matter," Slockett said." Slockett goes on to say, "The present prime suspect is not from the Iowa County area and has never lived in the area, but the individual did know one of the victims, and it was not a random killing.

The road taken has many persons of interest in this crime, but no solutions.

Chapter 11

The Mystery of the Vega

Scripture: *God will meet all your needs.*
—**Philippians 4:19**

There has been a mystery surrounding my car, a Spirit of America Chevrolet Vega. When Roger left for work on the morning of Monday, September 8, he drove my car while leaving me his Volkswagen Rabbit. I assumed that my car would remain parked in Savannah, Missouri, near his place of work until his return from his two-week work assignment in Kahoka, Missouri. That way, he would have a way home upon completion of that work assignment.

But that is not what happened with my car.

I have since learned that Roger took my car and left it with Rose to drive and drove her Chevrolet Malibu to work that morning. Before he left for Kahoka, he gave Rose's keys to Matt, a GTE coworker, and instructed him to park her car at his home until he returned from the job assignment. Sometime within those first couple of days, Matt got Rose's car back to her and exchanged it for my Vega.

Matt was interviewed by DCI Special Agent R.C. Benson on 9/14/80.

That report states, "Matt stated that he last talked to the victim on the telephone Tuesday, referring to September 9, 1980, when the victim called him at his residence. He stated that on Monday, September 8, 1980, at approximately 9:30 AM, he did talk to Roger regarding the car. The victim at that time gave him a set of car keys and advised him to take the car home with him because he was going to Kahoka, Missouri, to work on a telephone installation job. Matt stated that he drove the vehicle to his home and parked it in the driveway.

"Monday after work, Matt stated he returned the car because the victim had found that he was not leaving for Kahoka, but he was going to leave the following Monday, referring to September 15, 1980. On Tuesday afternoon, September 9, 1980, Roger called him at his residence and informed him to keep the car, but Matt informed him that he had already returned it. According to Matt, the victim advised that he didn't mean for him to go to all the trouble. Matt stated that this was the last time he ever talked to his coworker alive.

"Matt advised that this was a 1977 light blue Malibu which he later found to be the vehicle of Rose Burkert."

Matt was a relative by marriage. He had been to our house and around us enough to know what vehicles we drove. This piece of information on Matt's interview raises questions in my mind. Who did Matt think the Malibu belonged to? How did he know who to take the Malibu back to? Because later in the interview, Matt states,

"When asked by the reporting agent if he was aware of the identity of the female victim that his (relative and coworker) was with, Matt advised that he had heard from different individuals at work that his (relative) was seeing a Rose Burkert.

"(Matt) advised that his (relative) never informed him of the identity of this female, but he had heard from other employees that the female worked as a Nurse's Aide at the Shady Lawn Nursing Home in Savannah, Missouri."

Somehow, Matt returned the car and keys to Rose, whom he did not know, and got my Vega back from her. He and a fellow employee named Greg brought my Vega back to our house and parked it in the driveway on Tuesday, September 9, 1980.

When I checked on the house and picked up the mail, my car was back in the driveway. I wondered why Roger was back home before the two weeks were up. After checking the house and finding that Roger wasn't there, I was puzzled as to what was going on. I called Matt and asked him why my car was back in the driveway and Roger was not home. I don't remember Matt's excuse because I was still perplexed over what was happening. And to this day, I still don't understand the car situation because it does not make sense. Roger would need a way home when he returned from the two weeks of work in Kahoka, so why did Matt bring the car back to the house? There is the story that Matt said he did not bring my Vega back until the Monday after the murder. If that were the case, why would I call him to ask why the car was back? Also, he supposedly stated that he brought my car back because it was leaking oil on his driveway. To my knowledge, my Vega never leaked oil at that time or later.

I do not know if this car situation is important to the crime. I have always had a feeling that it did, but who knows? But it does point out discrepancies in interview information.

Chapter 12

Feelings

Scripture:" My God, my God, why hast thou forsaken me?"
—Matthew 27: 46

According to Swiss-American psychiatrist Katherine Kubler-Ross in her book *On Death and Dying*, there are five stages of grief.

I'm not sure if Ms. Kubler Ross explains that you can move from one stage to another all in one day. These stages do not have to be consecutive, but they could be. A person may go through all stages in a matter of minutes, a day, days, etc.

#1 Denial

In an earlier chapter, I said I was in denial when the detectives told me the news of Roger's death. I told them it could not be Roger because he was not in Iowa but Kahoka, Missouri. I told detectives that someone must have stolen his ID and that anytime he would call me to say he was alright, it was all a mistake. By all appearances to me and many others, Roger was a dedicated Christian man and husband. And because I trusted he was those two things, a devoted Christian man and husband, I did not question his love for God or me. And for him to be murdered with another woman, it just couldn't be true. I was asked by the detective if I knew a Rose Burkert. I had never heard of her--I had no idea who she was.

But Saturday night turned into Sunday, and by Sunday evening, Roger's brother had been to Iowa to identify his body. With Roger's death being verified, I was left with more questions than answers. Who was Rose, how did Roger meet her, and how long had their affair been going on? On and on went my questions, but law enforcement would not answer them. I eventually hired a private investigator to find the answers to my questions.

#2 Anger

I feel that I went through this stage briefly a couple of times. Rightly so, I should have been in this stage for a while. The first time I remember I was angry was a few days after the crime when a law enforcement officer brought Roger's suitcase back to me at my parents' house. I looked through the suitcase before the officer left and saw clothes that were not Roger's but Rose's. Her clothes did not belong in MY husband's suitcase among his clothes. How dare her clothes be in there with his. He was MY husband, NOT hers! There was a ditch that ran along the side of my parent's house. I promptly walked over to the ditch and threw her clothes into it. The officer retrieved her clothes, and I assume they were given to her relatives. My action was done out of anger toward Rose, and the situation I now found myself in was not created by me. But it was created by Roger and her.

The most cathartic time was in a dream. The first-year anniversary of the crime was approaching, and one night I had a dream. Earlier, I spoke about how Roger used to walk me home from school to my grandparents' house. So, in my dream, Roger and I were at my grandparents' house, and I was sitting on top of him as he lay on the kitchen floor, beating the crap out of him. It was after that point I felt I could move on with my life. For example, I felt I was ready to begin dating again.

After the murders, I sought counseling with my King Hill Baptist minister. I explained to him my anger over how Roger's death occurred. Why couldn't he have died in an accident in his GTE truck on the way to Kahoka? That way, I could have escaped the embarrassment of him being murdered with his girlfriend. Maybe I would never have known he had a girlfriend if it had happened that way.

#3 Bargaining

Why had this happened to me? Why did you let this happen to me, God? God, you could have just as easily made it an accident on the way to Kahoka. Why God, why? This was my bargaining portion with God. My pastor told me that it was good that I could vocalize my feelings to God. After all, God knows what we think, so he already knows our anger. Besides, he is a strong God and can take our wailings at him. And I was told we need to own our feelings and vocalize them to God to be able to accept what has happened to us and move on.

I was in a Bible Study many years later where the subject came up about my anger toward God for what had happened to us. Some of the attendees in the Bible Study were appalled at the thought that anger would be expressed toward God. I explained to them about the good counseling I had received from a former pastor. Also, I pointed out to them that when Jesus was on the cross, in Matthew 27: 46, he asked, "My God, my God, why hast thou forsaken me?" Even Jesus, as perfect as he was, questioned God.

The bargaining stage seems to fit more with people who are trying to come to terms with their own impending death, such as dying with some terminal illness such as cancer. The person may try to bargain with God to let them live long enough to see their child get married. Or long enough for some other life event to take place.

#4 Depression

After the confirmation that it was Roger who had been killed, I believe that I moved from the emotion of denial to depression. This heavy fog engulfed me and weighed me down. I had trouble eating, thinking, and moving. I remember very little about that time except for bits and pieces. A church friend brought me something to help me sleep. Also, the pastor Roger had gone to for counseling was one of the first people to come and see me. I asked him if Roger had talked to him about Rose when he went to him for counseling. He stated that he had. He said Roger was conflicted on what to do and felt that he was looking to him for affirmation for what he was doing. But, of course, he would not give him that affirmation. But he did speak prophetic words to Roger. He told Roger if he continued down the road he was going, it would destroy him. Of course, he was talking about Roger's spiritual witness and life. Little did he suspect in his wildest imagination that Roger would literally be destroyed. I feel God was trying to protect and warn Roger, but he was too wrapped up in his sin to heed the warning. The pastor explained to me that he could not divulge the information that Roger had confided in him before his death, but he saw no reason to withhold the information any longer since he was dead—another confirmation that this was not a dream, but indeed my new reality.

Another good piece of advice I would give to someone going through the death of a loved one. Find someone you can confide in and cry in front of at any time grief hits you. One time I remember that a few of my friends were with me to go to my house on King Hill. I sat in the car in our driveway--no, not *our* driveway; it was only *my* driveway now. There was no more *our* or *we*; it was just *my* and *me*. Here I was a *"lonely only"* again, which I hated. I sat in the car and lamented to my friends that my big two-story house would never house Roger and my children--never have our children laughing and playing there. In my depression, I grieved Roger, the married life I had with him and would never have again, children we never had or would ever have. Why God, why? The person I went to was my mom. She was there when I would break down and cry at a moment's notice. She didn't have to say much, just sit and listen. My mom had been my rock throughout my whole life, especially in my many times of grief over Roger. Her death in 2019 was quite hard because my rock was now gone.

#5 ACCEPTANCE

I think that a person can go in and out of this last stage as well as the other stages. Earlier, I likened grief to a wound. You think your grief wound has healed up, and then some memory or something comes along to open it. It bleeds again and hurts, and then the healing process starts all over again. But it doesn't seem to bleed as bad or as long. Time does have a way of helping us heal. However, I think I have been in and out of this stage for the last 40 years, and

I think that I still have not fully accepted it due to the case still being unsolved. Acceptance can be described as "moving on." In that sense, I moved on by remarrying, raising a child, and living again with joy. But I still feel like an albatross hangs around my neck since it is unsolved. If the crime were solved, I would not have justice, but I would at least have closure.

My journey on this life road has brought me through roadblocks of denial, anger, bargaining, depression, and acceptance to some degree.

Chapter 13

The Rest of the Story

Scripture: "To every thing there is a season, and a time to every purpose under the heaven: A time to be born, and a time to die ... A time to weep, and a time to laugh; a time to mourn, and a time to dance."
—Ecclesiastes 3:1, 2a, 4 KJV

The famous radio personality, Paul Harvey, would tell interesting stories and then end his program with, "And now you know the rest of the story." In this chapter, I will try to tell you "the rest of the story" as I know it.

In January 2019, I was contacted by a man named Mike Morford, a true-crime podcast host. He emcees two radio podcasts, *Criminology* and *A Murder in My Family*. He explained that he was doing a podcast on Roger's murder, and he wanted to talk with me. Several conversations later, Mike produced *Criminology—Episode 51, The Amana Hatchet Murders*, which aired the first of March 2019, and *A Murder in My Family—Episode 33, Roger Atkison*, which aired April 19, 2019. Mike later contacted a TV production company and recommended they try to do a TV show on the crime. See a list of questions at the end of this chapter that Mr. Morford asked me.

A television production company out of Los Angeles named Wilshire Productions was launching a new show, *The DNA of Murder*, with retired California criminal investigator Paul Holes, as the crime investigator of the show. They decided to have the launching program be a 90-minute special about Roger and Rose's murders. The TV program was filmed at various locations in Iowa and Missouri pertinent to the crime. I was privileged to be filmed in my home while being interviewed by Mr. Holes and Ms. Yolanda McClary. I hoped having the murders on a TV show would accomplish several purposes. First, it showed visuals of the motel room setup and actual photos of the crime scene. Those were photos I had never seen before. It also brought national attention to an unsolved murder of more than 40 years ago. DNA samples that the Iowa County Sheriff's office had taken were able to be assessed in a timely manner, and suspects were eliminated quicker.

One of the first things Mr. Holes asked me in his interview was who I suspected of committing Roger's murder. My first response was from someone who worked with Roger at General Telephone and Electronics Corporation (GTE). Some of his fellow workers knew where he was working the preceding week of his death (Kahoka, Missouri), and some of the men knew he was having Rose join him there at Kahoka and taking her to the Amana Colonies in Iowa on the weekend.

The next question Mr. Holes asked me was if I had suspected my dad of having anything to do with the murders. I did admit that I had suspected Dad due to his odd behavior that I went into in the chapter, *Elephant in the Room.*

The conclusion drawn at the end of the show by Mr. Holes and Ms. McClary was that my dad did not have anything to do with the murders. And they felt that the Amana murders could be connected to two other previous

Axed!

murders, one in Mississippi and the other in Illinois. The suspect in the Illinois murder was Raymundo Esparza, who died in 1983.

Mr. Holes felt that the facts that the Galesburg, Illinois, and Amana, Iowa, murders had in common were compelling.

The following are the similarities:
1. The weapons were both hatchet-type instruments;
2. Death by blows to the head;
3. Committed at well-known motels: Galesburg was the Sheraton Motel, Amana was Holiday Inn;
4. Toothpaste was squirted on the floor beside the victim in Galesburg, toothpaste was squirted in the bathtub in Amana;
5. Motels were off busy interstates: Galesburg I-74, Amana I-80;
6. Wallet contents were dispersed on the floor;
7. Rooms were on the second floor, in Galesburg, room 217; in Amana, room 260;
8. The bedspreads appeared to be used as a restraint.

The following are dissimilarities:
1. Sexual overtones in Galesburg murder; no evidence of that at Amana, Roger's body was further examined by the St. Joseph Buchanan County Coroner after it arrived in St. Joseph, and his findings were that there was no sign of homosexual activity to his body;
2. Galesburg one victim, Amana two;
3. Toothpaste squirted at Amana was done with force as if by a fist smashing it, Galesburg not done with force;
4. One perpetrator at Galesburg. It appears there were at least two at Amana;

5. The blows to the head were similar, but there were also wounds to other parts of the bodies at Amana, like to the arms, which were not similar;
6. Although at both locations, the contents of the male victim's wallets were dispersed on the floor, a picture of the male victim's niece was torn and thrown on the floor at Amana.

An interesting side note on the toothpaste issue: "The initial investigator (on the Galesburg case), retired Galesburg Police Department Lt. Robert Horton, told Holes he later consulted a forensic psychiatrist to gain insight into why an offender would squirt out toothpaste. 'Some heroin addicts, that's about the only way they can satisfy themselves,' Horton said. 'If an addict experiences erectile dysfunction, then ejaculation simulation is the 'only way they can achieve sexual gratification,' thus the squirting out of toothpaste to emulate their release of semen."

Another murder happened in Meridian, Mississippi, which has similarities to Kyle's murder in Galesburg. A man named Jack McDonald, 23, was also bludgeoned to death in the head with an ax-like instrument in 1970 at a Travel Inn motel in room 412 located on a major highway in Meridian, Mississippi. He was found in a bent-over position, such as Kyle, and the top of his body was covered up. Toothpaste had been squeezed into the toilet, and his wallet was missing.

There has been speculation that Esparza could have committed murders at all three locations. And at the end of the DNA of Murder TV show, it was told that the Iowa County Sheriff's office was prepared to have the body of Esparza exhumed for DNA comparisons. But at the time of this book going to press, it had not been done, and it is doubtful that will happen. Esparza is buried in California, and it would be a very expensive undertaking. Besides, the available identification articles from Esparza were tested against Amana DNA without success.

I admit that the similarities are many, but I must agree with Sheriff Slockett when he stated it was someone they knew and was personal. I don't feel the TV show brought us any closer to solving this murder. In many respects, I wished I hadn't participated in it. I was unhappy with the way things were going at the end of the filming of the TV show and wrote the following letter to the producer.

Cerise,

Yes indeed, the filming of your TV show has brought up unpleasant emotions and feelings. Thank you for acknowledging those feelings.

When Roger was murdered 39 years ago this coming week, I quickly learned to not trust reporters because no matter how clear they were told facts surrounding the case, they would usually report the news how they wanted it told regardless of how it affected the living victims.

And yes, I said living victims. On September 13, 1980, two dead victims were found at the Holiday Inn on I-80 in Iowa. Those of us who were family of Roger and Rose were left as living victims. My mom wrote a letter to DCI Agent Benson on March 24, 1993. Here's what she said: "We are pleased that you are still working to solve the case—but I do resent the way Marcie had been questioned without regard to her personal welfare. When she explained that she was facing surgery and did not feel like discussing the case without her husband present. I do think it unkind and unfeeling to not allow him to stay with her. You know there are times when a little moral support from someone who cares means a lot. Remember she was also a victim of a terrible tragedy in 1980. The only difference is—she survived."

Family are the victims now and have been for the last 39 years, and sometimes have suffered immensely at the mercy of those media people who want to profit at the expense of our privacy and sanity, as we grasped for answers and conclusion to this horrible tragedy.

Now I seriously question if I made a gross call in judgment in participation in your program. I trusted your production company with my openness to my home and our life, but feel I have not been honest and open with in return.

I was told on more than one occasion that Mr. Holes would report to me his ultimate findings, instead you state in your last email, "As you know (how did I know when Mr. Holes met with Sheriff Rotter, as I asked for a date and was not supplied with that information), Paul met for a final time in Los Angeles with Sheriff Rotter this past week and some new information came to light that might help close the gap on some of your lingering questions." Mr. Holes met for a final time with the Sheriff? Does that mean he solved the case? And how am I supposed to know that information when no one has contacted me to inform me of anything? Do I have to wait till the program airs to find out like everyone else?

I remember Mr. Holes saying that my dad did not kill Roger, but I do not remember him saying that Dad did not have anything to do with the murder. I was so emotionally wrought by that time, I should have asked more questions. If you remember, I was struggling with family betrayal saying Dad did have something to do with it.

Axed!

I realize that this is a job for all of you, a way to make a living, a way for Mr. Holes to promote his fame, but the people on the other end of your job/living are real humans with real emotions—living victims. Please think of what I have said in this letter when you deal with the next living victims.

Sincerely,
Marcella

In a day or so, I received a bouquet of flowers from the production crew.

The journey on this less traveled road has taken me down a road of various experiences and opportunities to meet interesting new people.

* * *

Radio Interview by Mike Morford

Here are the questions from Mike Morford and my responses:

Marcella, I host two podcasts; one is called *Criminology*. The other is called, *The Murder in My Family*. Both podcasts are a bit different from one another.

Criminology is a deep dive, investigative, detail-oriented coverage of the cases. We look at the facts, the clues, the evidence, the possible theories, and suspects. We include guest segments including family of victims, police investigators, witnesses, etc. We mostly cover cold and unsolved cases. Roger and Rose's murders would fit this show very well, and there is a lot to explore.

The Murder in My Family is more focused on the victim, their family, and their family's effort to get justice for their loved one. It's not as in depth as far as the background, and detailed information; it focuses more on the family member interview. I start each episode with a 10-minute or so back story of the case and the victim, and I follow it up with a longer 30–40-minute interview with the family member.

My guests for this show are family members of both solved and unsolved murders.

I have common goals for both of these shows. I want them to be accurate and correct as much as possible. Sometimes, as we discussed, not everything in the newspaper is correct. Having guests on that are family members, Detectives, etc., helps us to tell a more accurate and completely truthful story. We always treat these cases respectfully and with dignity for the victims and their families. It's important to me that you know that. The other goal is to help the families get justice for their loved ones. We want more people to hear about these cases and spread the word about them, talk about them, and share them on social media. That might lead to new tips or leads coming to the police. We reach over 100,000 people a month all over the United States (and the world).

Questions:
1. Please tell us about your husband, what kind of person was he, and what are some of your memories of him?

Answer: Roger was probably one of the friendliest people you'd meet. He almost always had an infectious smile. He was kind-hearted and loved children and animals. Family was important to him as he was one of seven

Axed!

children born to his parents. My fondest memory of him was riding all over the south part of the town we grew up in on a bicycle built for two that his older brother made.

2. As far as you know of, did he have any enemies that might want to hurt him?

Answer: I know of no enemies Roger might have had. Like I said earlier, he rarely met a stranger.

3. What was your interaction with police like right after the murders happened?

Answer: I was told about the murder by two St. Joseph, Mo. detectives. They asked a lot of questions, but gave me very little information. Throughout the years, the law enforcement division in Iowa, DCI (Division of Criminal Investigation), Iowa Sheriff, etc., have given me very little information. What I have learned about the murders has mostly been obtained from the media and the private investigator I hired.

4. (We have to touch on this because we need to have some explanation for listeners) I know this is a bit personal, but how is it that Roger & Rose came to be together in that hotel room? Were they having an affair, and if so, was the affair just as much of a shock as the murders?

Answer: When I hired a private investigator, he told me Roger and Rose started their affair when Roger, a GTE telephone repairman/installer, had a telephone job at Rose's house in June of 1980. Not only did I learn on Saturday, September 13, 1980, that my husband of seven years, and teenage sweetheart since I was 15½, was killed, but he was killed with another woman.

5. (This is sort of related to the last question) In many murder cases, especially one with these kinds of

circumstances, police will initially suspect jealousy and consider those closest to the victim as suspects. Did police ever question you for possibly being jealous of any kind of relationship between Roger and Rose, and if so, how difficult was that for you personally? Also, to your knowledge, did they ever question anyone that may have been jealous of Roger, perhaps someone that was romantically connected or interested in Rose?

Answer: I, of course, was questioned—took a lie detector test, etc. But the affair shocked me. I had what I thought was a Christian husband whom I trusted to be faithful to me. We regularly attended our church and served there. Roger's behavior came as a shock to most of the people who knew him, even his closest friends. It was like there were two Rogers: the Christian husband and the philandering one.

Rose had an ex-boyfriend, who I understand she had broken up with right before Roger. She went to the local county Sheriff's Office and told them if anything happened to her, to look to him. He had supposedly threatened her and killed and strung up her dog. **(I later learned that this story about the dog is false. The dog was found dead in a neighbor's driveway, but it appeared it had been run over.)**

6. Please tell us about what, if any, inaccuracies about your husband that were printed in newspapers or posted on the Internet.

Answer: I did not write any answers in my notes on this question.

7. How tough has this ordeal been on you and your family over the years?

Axed!

Answer: Unless you go through this sort of thing, you cannot imagine what it is like. Whenever there is a crime committed, there are the obvious victims of the case. But the survivors—spouses, parents, siblings, extended family—all are LIVING VICTIMS. I think the hardest thing is not having closure. To know who and why would be closure for me. But there never can be justice. There can never be justice because a husband/wife, son/daughter, brother/sister, aunt/uncle, etc., have been taken from their loved ones forever. But there can be closure.

8. Now, all of these years later, what's the status of the case—do police still regularly investigate it and keep you updated?
9. To your knowledge, is there any DNA or other physical evidence that might help to solve the case?

Answer to questions 8 & 9: I hear periodically from Sheriff Rob Rotter. The last I heard DNA was processed, but it didn't show anything.

10. (In every episode I ask the guest this, it's very important.) If someone out there listening in the audience has information, who should they contact? (You can share the police contact info.)

Answer: Sheriff Robert Rotter (319) 642-7307; iowacounty.iowa.gov; rrotter@iowacosheriff.org; Iowa County, 960 Franklyn, Marengo, Iowa 52301

11. Lastly, I would just like you to run through the case as you see it and understand it, from the time leading up to the murder, the murder itself, to the aftermath and investigation. Then I can use all of the details you provide to help tell the story accurately and completely.

Note: Since the podcasts are archived, you, the reader, can go back and listen to these podcasts to hear the rest of the information.

Epilogue:

The Difference

Scripture: "And we know that all things work together to them that love God, to them who are called according to his purpose."
—Romans 8:28.

I am a better, stronger woman because of the road I chose back in 1970, over fifty years ago. It has been filled with love, adventure, heartache, peace, and many more attributes too numerous to mention. It has been filled with people dear to my heart such as my husband Vernie, daughter Corey Lynn, my three precious granddaughters; Ava Lynn, Tracy Alivia, and Addison Rose, as well as numerous other new friends who otherwise may not have been in my life had I chose the other road.

One evening on the very popular zombie TV series, *Walking Dead*, the character Father Gabriel made a statement about being on the "right path" even if they were all on the "wrong road." "What?" I asked myself. "How can you be on the wrong road but the right path?" But after pondering that jewel of a statement from Father Gabriel, I feel I can say the *difference* for me is that I have been on the right path *AND* the right road for the past 70 years of my life as God has intended for me to be on. I can say as

Robert Frost did in his poem, but say it differently, "When my two roads took off into entirely different directions, that right road and right path that I chose have made all the difference in my life."

A good, **God blessed difference**....

Thank You, and praise you, God!

Discussion questions:

Prologue
1. Have you ever felt like you were "falling off a cliff"? What feelings did that conjure up for you?
2. Can a Christian be active in many facets of volunteer work in the church and still do wrong things?

Chapter 1.
1. Has God ever taken you where you did not want to go? If so, where was that?
2. Is there any part of Marcella's life you can identify with? If you can, what part is that?
3. Have you ever felt like you should have chosen a different life path? If so, what would it have been?

Chapter 2.
1. Have you ever questioned God on an issue in your life like Marcella?
2. Do you feel it is appropriate to question God?

Chapter 3.
1. Have you ever left home and then returned to live with your parents? If so, what kind of problems and feelings did that cause?

Axed!

2. What are your thoughts on the statement Marcella makes, "Sometimes when we are rebellious to God, I think he just steps back and lets us reap the rewards of our actions as a parent has to do with their own child."?
3. What do you think about telling God you are angry about something that has happened to you? Did Marcella's pastor give good advice to her, in your opinion?

Chapter 4.
1. Considering Roger's upbringing in a Christian home, do you think he conducted his life according to it?
2. What do you think was Roger's problem, that he was having numerous affairs during his marriage to Marcella? Could it have been from a lack of self-esteem or the opposite of too much ego?

Chapter 5.
1. Why do you think Rose's family would not share with Marcella? After all, they were victims of this crime too.
2. What are some facts you would like to know about Rose?

Chapter 6.
1. Do you think comparing this experience to a wound is a good analogy?
2. What do you think was the rest of the erased message on the bathroom door beside the word "this"? Why do you think it was written?

Chapter 7.
1. Do you think Marcella has really moved on?
2. Has Marcella been blessed over the years?

Chapter 8.
1. Do you think Marcella handled her harasser correctly?
2. How would you have handled the situation?

Chapter 9.
1. How do you think Marcella feels about her dad being a suspect?
2. Do you think her dad committed the crime or hired it done?
3. What do you think Marcella's feelings are about having an uncle as a serial killer?
4. If a relative such as her uncle or dad committed the crime, do you think she should ever find out the truth? Or is it better she never really knows the truth?

Chapter 10.
1. Who seems the most likely person of interest and why?
2. Could there be someone else not mentioned?

Chapter 11.
1. Do you think Marcella's Vega car played some role in the murder, or was it just a weird coincidence?
2. If you think it did play a role, what was it?

Chapter 12.
1. Have you ever experienced the five stages of grief? Talk about your feelings.
2. Do you feel Marcella has reached "acceptance" of Roger's murder? Why or why not?

Chapter 13.
1. Do you think Mr. Holes' conclusion on who committed the murder is correct?
2. Do you think Marcella should have done the television show? Why or why not?

Epilogue
1. Do you think Marcella has really found peace with the road she chose?
2. Defend your opinion.

Note: If this book is used as a Book Study, I would like to receive your thoughts on the discussion questions.
Please email your thoughts to me at:
marcellahatcheratkison@gmail.com

Thank you for reading my life story. I hope you have been truly blessed by reading it.

Made in the USA
Monee, IL
10 February 2025